veryday Abstract Conditional Reasoning

Everyday Abstract Conditional Reasoning

in Light of a 2,400 Year-Old Mistake in Logic

András Veszelka

Pellea Humán Kutató és Fejlesztő Bt.

Published by Pellea Humán Kutató és Fejlesztő Bt., Kecskemét, Hungary

www.pellea.hu

ISBN 978-963-08-9463-0

I am grateful to Professor László Bernáth for opening up his courses to allow the experiments reported in this book to take place. It happened twice that I headed in the wrong direction, and my experiments did not yield the expected results. But even then, he was patient and let me keep trying. I have learned that the problem is never when we are going in the wrong direction; the problem is when we give up trying.

Contents

1 Introduction

The conditional statement is a glaring example of how the abstractions of logic and people's 'everyday' reasoning deviate from each other. Many interpret this as a difference between formal and natural languages (see, for example, Copi, 1982). This differentiation can be traced back to the beginning of the 20th century, where, for example, Frege (1918-19/1984) argued that the difference between the interpretations of the conditional statement as prescribed in formal, mathematical logic and as used in 'everyday life' reveals linguistic or psychological components. This is where, with formal logic as a normative background, the search for these linguistic or psychological components deemed different from logic began: first, in the philosophy of language, then in linguistics and finally, in psychology.

However, the so-called everyday interpretation of the conditional statement does not merely deviate from such mathematically-oriented formal languages as propositional logic (Whitehead & Russell, 1910-13/1962), which originated in Frege's era and which soon became the predominant logic of the 20th century, but also from the classical Greco-Roman/scholastic interpretation of the conditional statement. This interpretation is basically the same as that of propositional logic, but it has been clearly extracted from natural language in a linguistic, philosophical and psychological environment as distinct from a mathematical environment. This is not affected by the fact that from the 19th century on, mathematicians also began to use the same abstraction. This means that the discrepancy between the everyday interpretation and the classical abstraction exists within the same system. In other words, contrary to the views of Frege, everyday reasoning, in all of its forms, is directly relevant when evaluating the correctness of the classical interpretation. Perhaps the classical abstraction was simply mistaken, and by fixing it, logic and everyday reasoning immediately become much more compatible with each other.

2 Historical considerations

2.1 THE ABSTRACTION ERROR IN CLASSICAL LOGIC

That said, when looking back to the classical interpretation, it can be seen that it is indeed erroneous. Instead of the 'if P then Q' statement, classical logicians have erroneously abstracted the 'if P or R then Q' statement. Let's take an example from Jevons (1906, p. 70), a late scholastic logician:

'If the snow is mixed with salt, it melts.'

As is well known, in this 'if P then Q' statement from the 'snow being mixed with salt' (P) antecedent, it is correct to infer the 'snow melts' (Q) consequent (modus ponens, (MP)). Also, from the 'snow not melting' (not-Q) it is correct to infer that 'it has not been mixed with salt' (not-P) (modus tollens, (MT)).

However, the denial of the antecedent (DA), 'if the snow is not mixed with salt (not-P), it does not melt (not-Q)' and the affirmation of the consequent (AC), 'if the snow melts (Q), it was mixed with salt (P)', are incorrect. Jevons has argued that in the case of the DA inference from the 'snow not mixed with salt' (not-P), it does not follow that 'it does not melt' (not-Q) because it can melt by other means as well. For the same reason, we cannot endorse the AC inference. It is impossible to find any other explanation, even going back several hundred years, as to why these two latter inferences are incorrect. On the contrary, this interpretation can be traced back to Aristotle, who wrote that:

> The refutation, which depends upon the consequent, arises because people suppose that the relation of consequence is convertible. For whenever, suppose A is, B necessarily is, they then suppose also that if B is, A necessarily is. This is also the source of the deceptions that attend opinions based on sense perception. For people often suppose bile to be honey because honey is attended by a yellow colour: also, since after rain the ground is wet in consequence, we suppose that if the ground is wet, it has been raining; whereas that does not necessarily follow (Aristotle, 1928, 167b1ff).

To complete this argument, the inference that it has been raining does not necessarily follow because there are other possible means to make the ground wet. However, if we refer to additional possible causes, that is, to additional possible antecedents during the abstractions, these have to be denoted. In logic, it is fundamental to restrict ourselves to explicitly stated premises (Evans & Over, 2004, p. 6). With their denotation, however, it can be seen that with the above explanations, we characterised the 'if P or R then Q' statement. Jevons's (1906) example was, therefore, the 'If the snow is mixed with salt or, for example, the sun is shining, the snow melts' statement that he erroneously characterised in terms of P and Q only.

2.2   THE CORRECT ABSTRACTION OF THE CONDITIONAL STATEMENT

The question arises, therefore, of what the correct abstraction of the conditional statement can then be, specifically, the abstraction of the relationship in which there is no wedging 'or R' component. I believe the correct inference pattern is the equivalence, in which all the MP, MT, AC and DA inferences are valid.

For example, we endorse the equivalent AC and DA inferences for the 'if-then' connective even in the case of the extended, 'If the snow is mixed with salt or the sun is shining, the snow melts' (if P or R then Q) statement. From 'the snow melts' (Q), we endorse the affirmation of the consequent (AC) inference, and we deduce to 'the snow was mixed with salt or the sun is shining' (P or R). As the traditional interpretation of the conditional statement goes, only *within this* do we not infer exclusively P because it can also be R. This correspondence can also be demonstrated in the same way in the case of the other three classical inferences. On the other hand, classical equivalent statements such as, for instance, 'if it is a man, it is a risible thing' (Boethius, before 522/1988, p. 136) were viewed as equivalent because, as far as ancient logicians were concerned, the context of these statements did not allow them to wedge any alternative antecedent. That is, to refer back to Aristotle's citation above, the correct interpretation of the conditional statement is to assume that the 'relation of consequence is convertible', and to assume not only that Q necessarily follows from P, but also that P necessarily follows from Q. This whole book will be devoted to convince the reader of this logic.

Table 1. The truth table of the conditional statement and the equivalence/

biconditional[*]

		Conditional	Equivalence/biconditional
P	Q	If P then Q	If and only if P then Q
True	True	True	True
True	False	False	False
False	True	True	False
False	False	True	True

[*]It can be seen that the truth values of the conditional statement and the equivalent relation, or, to use another term, the biconditional, can be equated with scholastic logic. When the conditional statement is true, which is the starting point in the scholastic interpretation, then P can co-occur with Q only; that is, in scholastic terms, one can infer from P to Q (MP inference). Similarly, not-Q can co-occur only with not-P, which means that from not-Q, one has to infer not-P (MT inference). In addition, in the truth table of the biconditional, Q must also co-occur with P and not-P with not-Q. However, this need not be fulfilled in the truth table of the conditional statement, which means that the affirmation of the consequent and the denial of the antecedent are valid inferences only in the case of the biconditional relation.

In the 20th century, instead of scholastic or Greco-Roman logic, Whitehead and Russell's (1910-13/1962) propositional logic was primarily used as a referential background when presenting and analysing the conditional inferences. In this mathematical logic, the interpretation of the conditional statement, although presented in a different form, is basically identical to the ancient interpretation. This interpretation is often displayed in the form of a truth table, as shown in Table 1.

In the past century, many proponents of propositional logic described such similarities between propositional logic and the classical Greco-

Roman logic as mere coincidence. Interestingly, it is not only truth values that somehow coincide with the erroneous ancient abstraction. Propositional logic itself refers to the undenoted alternative antecedents when it differentiates the equivalence or biconditional with the artificial expression '*if and only if* P then Q' from the 'if P then Q' conditional. In the latter case, by parity of argument, several antecedents can lead to Q.

It is often quite difficult to explain the truth values of propositional logic to laypeople, and to facilitate this, Geis and Zwicky (1971) reinvented and employed the aforementioned Greco-Roman interpretation. By mentioning alternative antecedents to their pupils, they managed to block one of the most common fallacies that people commit in the case of the conditional statement—the equivalent or biconditional inferences.

Subsequently, researchers such as Rumain, Connell and Braine (1983); Markovits (1985); Byrne (1989); or Cummins, Lubart, Alksnis and Rist (1991) have implemented this approach in psychology and have experimentally verified its basic mechanism. In doing so, Byrne also demonstrated that if in an 'if P then Q' statement, the second antecedent is connected to the initial antecedent with an 'and' connective, then in terms of P and Q only, the MP and MT inferences would be invalid and the DA and AC inferences would remain valid. This is the case, for instance, in the 'If the snow is mixed with salt and it is not extremely cold, it melts' (If P and R then Q) statement.

These are very interesting relationships, however, and as a consequence of the historical reasons illustrated in the Introduction, this phenomenon is interpreted in linguistics and in psychology as a semantic or pragmatic effect, which is contrary to logic. It was nevertheless demonstrated above that this phenomenon is actually the update of the ancient logical interpretation of the conditional statement. It is the exact definition of what differentiates between the two well-known inference patterns on the conditional statement, the traditionally accepted conditional inference pattern, which allows only MP and MT, and the equivalence.

In ancient logic, after several hundred years of thinking, the rule of thumb finally used was that since the conditional statement can evoke both conditional and equivalent inferences, one should label only those inferences that are prescribed by both of them as valid; that is, the MP and the MT (see Maróth, 1983, in Hungarian, or directly in Boethius, before 522/1988, p. 136). Obviously, the new definition is more accurate. Boethius is called 'the tutor of the Middle Ages' because he had the largest influence on the logic of this period—medieval scholastic logic (Gál, 1979). Scholastic logic remained the predominant logic up until the birth of mathematical logic, and most importantly, until Frege's (1879) *Begriffsschrift* and Whitehead and Russell's propositional logic, published in their *Principa Mathematica* (Whitehead & Russell, 1910-13/1962) that, as discussed above, coincidentally implemented the very same abstraction.

2.2.1   Two mathematical examples

Since there is a strong interpretative separation today between mathematical logic and ancient logic, it must be noted that although we have discussed the conditional statement so far through examples from the field of humanities, those mentioned above can be, of course, demonstrated with mathematical examples as well. Let us take the following example:

'If a number is even, it is an integer.'

According to the traditional interpretation of the conditional statement, from a number being an integer (Q), it does not follow that it is an even number (P) (that is, the AC inference does not hold), and from a number not being an even number (not-P), it does not follow that it is not an integer (not-Q) (that is, the DA inference does not hold, either).

Yet according to the approach propagated here, these inferences are valid. This might seem absurd, given that odd numbers are also integers. However, odd numbers have not been denoted above. We therefore have two options. We can choose not to take into account the odd numbers (which are a third, 'R' component), thereby completely ignoring them during the characterisation and endorsing the aforementioned seemingly absurd inferences. Our other option is to take them into account, but in doing so, we then have to denote them and characterise the following statement:

'If a number is even or odd, it is an integer.'

I believe there is no third option. Taking into account a proposition and not denoting it is against the basic principle of logic, which is even more fundamental than the abstraction of the connectives.

If one wishes to use a notation in which it is differentiated what has been explicitly stated and what was only general background knowledge, the 'or odd' component in the above sentence can be put in parentheses.

Tarski (1946/1995, p. 32) had a similar example to refute the general equivalent interpretation of the conditional statement. He wrote that the statement

'If x is a positive number, then 2x is a positive number.'

can be interpreted as an equivalence, but the equivalent interpretation cannot be a general rule, because replacing 2x with x^2 in this sentence already produces a relationship to which the classical interpretation of the conditional applies.

However, once again, if we were to ask Tarski why this is so, he would undoubtedly say that this is because the square of a negative number is also a positive number. As above, this is again a third, undenoted component. Therefore, once again, we either denote this component and then characterise this more compound sentence, or we do not denote this component, but then we have to endorse the seemingly fallacious equivalent inferences.

2.2.2   The tradition of undenoted components

Some might argue that the traditional interpretation of the conditional statement simply leaves open whether or not alternative antecedents can appear on the left side of the conditional statement. This would, in fact, be consistent with Boethius's (before 522/1988) or Tarski's (1946/1995) aforementioned interpretations.

However, such components can also appear on the right side. Let us take again our initial example sentence:

'If the snow is mixed with salt, it melts.'

In this statement, we can add to the consequent, using the 'and' and the 'or' connectives, that 'and there remain grains of salt on the ground' (S1) or that 'or the salt remains simply on its surface' (S2). These would also influence the endorsed inferences. For example, from the snow being mixed with salt (P), it does not necessarily follow that it melts (Q), if the salt can simply remain on the surface of the snow (S2) as well; therefore, in terms of P and Q only, the MP does not hold any longer. We have no reason to refer to possible additional components on the left side but completely ignore them on the right side.

A further problem is that on the left, as already mentioned in Section 2.2, the second antecedent can also be connected to the initial antecedent with an 'and' connective, not merely with an 'or' connective. In such a case, the extended conditional statement will evoke just the opposite inference pattern in terms of P and Q. As soon as we decide to incorporate these obvious other possibilities into the traditional abstraction, still trying to express the complete relation only in terms of P and Q, as is customary, the abstraction will completely lose its sense. With the traditional practice of referring to possible additional components only on the left and only as connected to the initial antecedent with an 'or' connective, at least some functioning of logic is preserved.

The solution to this dilemma is, of course, to simply denote every proposition, either on the left or on the right, if it is taken into account, or not to take it into account if it is not denoted. It seems hard to justify a logical abstraction in which we denote only some of the components and not others, and yet, this has been the practice in mainstream logic for the last 2,400 years.

2.3 EQUIVALENCE AND PRAGMATIC INFERENCES

Many things follow from the observations discussed above. One is that, contrary to what is generally assumed, it is not the equivalent relation that is formed from the sum of the two conditional statements 'if P then Q' and 'if Q then P' (hence the term bi-conditional, an expression which is therefore mainly avoided in this book). Instead, it is the traditional inference pattern of the conditional that emerges from the basic equivalent relationship when an alternative antecedent is added. Among others, this difference also affects theories on the conditional statement in natural languages.

Geis and Zwicky (1971), for example, explain the frequent equivalent interpretation of the 'if P then Q' statement in everyday life by saying that it invites the additional 'if not-P then not-Q' conditional statement, creating the equivalent inference pattern. According to the authors, this is a 'tendency of the human mind' (p. 562), a sort of Gricean implicature which is evaded only when people have reason to assume that the equivalent interpretation of the conditional statement is incorrect. Although the authors mention only alternative antecedents to their pupils to make them reason to reject the equivalent inferences and to make them infer according to the traditional inference pattern, they do not denote these components. Instead, they interpret the phenomenon as the effect of non-logical, pragmatic inferences on the basic logical inferences.

Horn (2000) argues in a similar way, claiming that people transform the sufficient relationship expressed in the traditional conditional statement into a stronger sufficient and necessary relationship. The former means that P is sufficient to evoke Q, but Q can also be evoked without P; the latter means that P is both sufficient and necessary to evoke Q, that is, P is a prerequisite for Q. Horn attempts to give a non-logical, pragmatic interpretation of this phenomenon. As outlined above, however, all of this can be described in terms of scholastic logic in a much simpler way. Particularly as in the sufficient-necessary distinction, which is frequently used in the psychological literature as well (e.g. Pollard, 1982; Thompson, 1995; Evans & Over, 2004, to mention just a few), 'sufficient' means, by definition, that alternative components are also present, although again without denoting them. In the same way, 'pragmatics' means, by definition, the contribution of context to meaning, and in this specific case, to inferences. It is therefore an obvious option to denote them.

The additional components are left undenoted by the assumption that logical consequences must always be valid, and they cannot be modified by additional components (see, for example, Oaksford & Chater, 2010). In other words, they are monotonic. Consequently, as it is assumed, if these content and context effects render previous consequences invalid, they cannot be logical, and so, as discussed in the Introduction, they are semantic, pragmatic or psychological.

As described above, however, after taking a closer look at the way the conditional statement has been abstracted in ancient logic, such a distinction cannot be maintained. The equivalent inference pattern does not contain a mixture of logical and non-logical components, whereas the traditional inference pattern, deemed 100% logical in these accounts, has both denoted and undenoted (or, as they are quite controversially interpreted today, logical and non-logical) components.

An easy way out of this interpretative problem is to simply denote all components that are taken into account, making them all 'logical'. Nowadays, specific non-monotonic logics are created precisely to handle such defeasible inferences. Still, the simplest non-monotonic logic arises by merely putting aside the monotonic interpretation of logic and simply denoting the additional instances if and when they emerge. In a non-technical way, this book follows this practice and will discuss many examples of the benefits of this simple method.

2.4   WHEN EXPERIMENTAL-BASED AND INSIGHT-BASED
RESEARCH MEET EACH OTHER

The analysis of the conditional statement on the basis of insight, as seen above, is customary in philosophical logic and linguistics. With today's convergence of the branches of sciences, this method intersects more and more with incorporating the results of the experiments conducted in psychology. In psychology, these experimental results are principally assumed to be similarly exact and as free of subjective influences as those in the natural sciences. These experiments are understood to be able to empirically verify or falsify hypotheses, and in this specific case, to verify or falsify our hypothesis that people in everyday life basically interpret the conditional statement as an equivalent relationship, and that this modifies into the traditionally accepted conditional inference pattern when an alternative antecedent is added.

It was already mentioned in the Introduction that the abstraction of the conditional statement was made in a philosophical, linguistic, psychological context. The ancient methodology of these sciences to verify their assumptions was based merely on insight, and we followed this procedure in the previous sections. However, today's experiments in human sciences also provide an empirical way, which allows testing these insights in a more objective manner. Since both the initial abstraction and the empirical testing procedures are within the framework of human sciences, it is valid to test the former with the latter. We simply underpin our insight-based assumptions with empirical support.

Another option to test the updated scholastic interpretation of the conditional statement is by investigating how it performs in a logical system, and a third is by addressing how it can handle the various dilemmas raised with regard to the traditional interpretation of the conditional statement in human sciences. To an extent, all of these will be discussed in this book, but the primary focus will be on the experiments and the theoretical/philosophical issues, since a very effective description can be given for them without the need to enter into logical technicalities.

In the following sections, we will therefore examine the picture that the predominant psychological experiments reveal about the everyday interpretation of the conditional statement. A great number of such experiments have been conducted in the past 50 years. Currently, the results of most of them appear to be in conflict with the approach propagated here. In fact, these results are summarily viewed as serious evidence against the applicability of logic in the characterisation of everyday conditional inferences. However, as this book will suggest, this perspective is merely the result of unsystematic research. By running some long-missing experiments, the basic equivalent interpretation of the conditional statement and the effect of the alternative antecedents can both be demonstrated.

3   The experimental investigation of the conditional statement

3.1   ABSTRACT TASKS

The most important experimental task with the most contradictory result is the 'single most investigated problem in the literature on deductive reasoning' (Evans, 1996, p. 224), Wason's (1966, 1968) abstract selection task. In this task, participants are shown four schematic cards and are told that these cards have a letter on one side and a number on the other. Participants are then asked what card or cards they would turn over in order to decide whether, for example, the 'If there is a letter E on one side, there is a number 4 on the other side' conditional statement is true. On the cards, the 'E' (P), 'K' (not-P), '4' (Q) and '7' (not-Q) can be seen. In this task, abstract letters and numbers are used in order to ensure that the context and the content have no influence on the results, and so the task accurately displays how people interpret the 'if-then' connective itself. The traditional conditional interpretation would involve selecting the cards P and not-Q, since these could have such instances on the other side that could falsify the conditional statement, while the biconditional interpretation would involve the selection of all four cards, since all instances could have a falsifying instance on the other side (see Table 1). The customary response is, however, merely the P and Q values.

In the psychological field of logical reasoning, the logical negation is expressed in three different ways. It can be implicit (such as the letter 'A' and its negation, 'K'); explicit (the letter 'A' and its negation, 'not-A'); and dichotomous, which is the same as the implicit, but in which the task instruction states that only two possible values can be found for the given term (for example, the letter 'A' and its negation, 'K'). In the selection task, the result is P and Q with all three negatives (see, for instance, Johnson-Laird & Wason, 1977). This bizarre, logically unidentifiable result constitutes an important basis for most of the theories in the field, such as for the mental models theory (Johnson-Laird & Byrne, 1991), for the information gain theory (Oaksford & Chater, 1998), or for the recent logical, non-monotonic approach of Stenning and van Lambalgen (2008).

There are three additional main tasks:

- The truth table task (e.g. Evans, 1972), in which the given co-occurrences in the four lines of the truth table of propositional logic (as shown in Table 1)—for example, the co-occurrence of 'not-P and not-Q' (line 4 in Table 1)—must be evaluated in terms of whether they verify or falsify the conditional statement, or they are irrelevant to it.

- The simple inference task (e.g. Rumain, Connell & Braine, 1983), in which, on the basis of the provided 'if P then Q' conditional statement, people must decide if the given conclusions follow from the minor premises or not, such as, for instance, whether or not from not-P, not-Q follows.

- The inference production task (e.g. Byrne, 1989), in which participants themselves write down what follows from the minor premises.

The available results that I found in the literature from the combination of these four main tasks and the three types of negatives are shown in Table 2.

As can be seen in Table 2, although there are biconditional solutions, the results are generally inconsistent, and there are missing data. For this reason, I have retested all tasks (Veszelka, 2007)[1]. In addition, since the results were already very robust for the abstract selection task for all three types of negatives, I also tested two so-called thematic problems in the selection task. In these problems, the conditional statements were embedded into an evidently biconditional context in order to determine if the results of these tasks deviate from the results of the abstract selection task, or if they also evoke the bizarre preference of the P and Q values instead of the selection of all cards, as was already observed once by Cheng, Holyoak, Nisbett and Oliver (1986). My abstract task results are shown in Table 3.

As can be seen, the most frequent response is the biconditional. Although there are alternative explanations (see Barouillet & Lecas, 1998; Evans, Clibbens & Rood, 1996; Evans & Over, 2004), the reasoning contained in the defective truth tables[2] can also be explained by assuming

---

[1] This paper was published in Hungarian. Its English version is available upon request.

[2] In the defective truth table, the co-occurrence of 'P and Q' verifies the conditional statement, the co-occurrence of 'P and not-Q' falsifies it and the 'not-P and Q' and the 'not-P and not-Q' co-occurrences are irrelevant to it.

Table 2. The most frequent responses on the main abstract task types with the three types of negatives

	Implicit negatives	Explicit negatives	Dichotomous negatives
Selection task	P&Q	P&Q	P&Q
Truth table task	Defective truth table[*]	Defective truth table/ Biconditional?[*]	Biconditional (83%)[†]
Simple inference task	Biconditional (48%)[‡]	?	Biconditional (60%)[‡]
Inference production task	?	?	Biconditional (92%)[†]

[*]Evans, Clibbens, and Rood (1996) – The authors did not report the complete response patterns but only the rate of individual inferences. The defective truth table is still obvious with implicit negatives, but in case of explicit negatives, the most frequent response could be both the defective truth table and the biconditional.
[†]George (1992)
[‡]Wagner-Egger (2007)

that the participants in these tasks interpret the conditional statement to refer to enumerations. Such an interpretation is not excluded in the task instruction, and it can be hypothesised to modify the initial equivalent connection between the propositions. Examining the case of enumerations, one can see, for example, that in the 'If you go to movie theatre P, you can watch movie Q' statement, if someone is going to a different movie theatre (not-P), nothing follows with regard to which movies the person can watch there (Q or not-Q?). In such cases, on the surface, we deduce only from the affirmed antecedent in exactly the same way as with the defective truth table.

Evans and Over (2004) mention several less central experimental tasks in which the results have a tendency toward such a defective truth table. They conclude that the reason for this could be that alternative components are taken into account, which is compatible with the 'enumerative' interpretation suggested here. In our present example, the alternative components are the different movie theatres, which are not necessarily influenced

Table 3. My results on the most frequent responses on the main abstract task types with the three types of negatives (Veszelka, 2007)

	Implicit negatives	Explicit negatives	Dichotomous negatives
Selection task	P&Q	P&Q	P&Q
Truth table task	Defective truth table	Defective truth table	Biconditional (50%)
Simple inference task	Defective truth table	Defective truth table	Biconditional (42%)
Inference production task	Biconditonal (73.3%)	Biconditional (52%)	Biconditional (67%)

by each other regarding their schedules. This 'enumerative' interpretation can therefore emerge the same way in the abstract truth table and simple inference tasks with implicit negatives, and can emerge even with explicit negatives, where people can revert the explicit negatives back to imaginary implicit negatives. However, in a dichotomous setting, where there are indeed only two possible variants for the antecedent and the consequent, the cases with a negative antecedent already reveal the truth values generated by the 'if-then' connective itself, and the equivalent answers do appear. We will discuss how the basic equivalent interpretation transforms into the 'enumerative' interpretation in more detail later in this book, when addressing the Raven paradox in Section 5.5.

Regarding the P and Q preference in the abstract selection task, the two tested definitely biconditional selection tasks also evoked this preference instead of biconditional responses. Consequently, this same preference in the abstract selection task does not disprove the basic biconditional interpretation.

According to my hypothesis (Veszelka, 1999, 2007), which has also been formulated and partially tested by Wagner-Egger (2007), in the selection task, people avoid the biconditional response of selecting all cards. They believe that selecting all four cards would be contrary to the task instruction, which, in fact, requires them to select *from among* the cards. This is fairly apparent in the case of the following task, which was one of the tasks involving biconditional context that I tested:

On one side of each card, there is the name of a city, and on the other side, there is a mode of transportation. Let us suppose that when someone goes to Budapest, he always goes by car, and when he goes to Szeged, he always goes by train. Likewise, when he travels by car, he always goes to Budapest, and when he travels by train, he always goes to Szeged. Mark the card or cards that must be turned over in order to decide whether this is true.

The following statements were printed on the cards: 'going to Budapest', 'going to Szeged', 'going by train' and 'going by car' (Veszelka, 2007, Exp. 3).

In this task, which was tested on 2 x 20 participants, everyone produced the biconditional answer in the inference production task, but only 10% did so in the selection task. However, as can be seen, the task was actually a pseudo-problem because it contained a clear description of what follows from what, or what value has to figure on the other side of the cards.

I also obtained the same result on the second clearly biconditional problem that I tested, the so-called 'ball-light' problem (Legrenzi, 1970). This task was stated as follows:

> There is a ball on a rail that can roll either to the left or to the right. If it takes one direction, it switches on a red light; if it moves in the other direction, it switches on a blue light. The directions of the ball and the results are shown on four cards. One side of each card shows the direction taken by the ball; the other side shows the colour of the light switched on.

> Suppose that if the ball moves to the left, it switches on the red light.

> Choose the card or cards that must be turned over in order to decide whether this statement is true.

The cards contained the phrases: 'moves to the left', 'moves to the right', 'switches on the red light' and 'switches on the blue light', respectively (Veszelka, 2007, Exp. 1).

This second problem is commonly accepted in the literature as a biconditional problem which, being tested on 2 x 30 participants, produced biconditional answers in 97% in inference production task, but only in 23% in selection task (Veszelka, 2007, Exp. 1). Even this 23% occurred for the response 'any' and not for the normally equivalent response 'all', which was selected in a mere 7%.

It is worth discussing in detail this 'any' response. Of course, in the ball-light selection task, this response is the correct solution: In the city-travel task above, cities and modes of transportation can combine in various ways, and it is possible, for example, that the person travels to both cities by car; however, in this ball-light problem, the context is partly hard-wired in the instruction, as a light can be connected to one direction only, and vice versa. Since there is hence a compulsory one-by-one correspondence between the lights and the paths, this inevitably creates a biconditional context; the only question is whether the biconditional relation arises from the left direction being exclusively linked to the red light, or whether the opposite is true and the right direction is linked to the red light. As both possibilities cover a biconditional relation, depicting exactly the opposite of each other in each case, the participants have only to decide whether the relation that holds is the one specified in the conditional statement of the task, or the other one, which the context of the task still allows. This requires turning over only one card, whichever it is.

Since participants are instructed to select a *specific* card or cards, this 'any' response can also be an avoided response. This was confirmed in one of my unpublished experiments, where participants solving this thematic ball-light selection task were given a list with possible answers including, and hence validating, the response 'any'. When participants had to select their responses from this list, the rate of 'any' responses increased from

20% to 60%, which was a significant difference with Pearson Chi-Square (1, 30) = 5.000, $p < .025$ and Cramer's V = .408. Although the 'all' response option was also included in the list, no participant selected it.

In this unpublished experiment, I also attempted to facilitate the 'all' response for the traditional abstract selection task by using the very same response list. This, however, did not significantly increase the rate of this equivalent response (the increase was from 13% to 33% on 2 x 15 participants, with a Pearson Chi-Square (1, 30) = 1.677, $p < .195$ and Cramer's V = .236, and from 0% to 13% when the experiment was repeated in another unpublished experiment on another set of 2 x 15 participants, with a Pearson Chi-Square (1, 30) = 2.143, $p < .143$ and Cramer's V = .267). No participant selected the response 'any' in this task.

Whereas this could suggest that the lack of 'all' selections in the abstract selection task cannot be explained by the simple avoidance of this response, I also tested the effect of this response list on the other evidently biconditional, thematic problem discussed above, where Hungarian cities were exclusively connected to modes of transportation. Whereas in this thematic task, the 'all' response is evidently the correct response, as the task is nothing other than a full description of an equivalent relationship, the rate of 'all' responses was not significantly increased when this option was included in the list of possible responses. In this condition, the rate of 'all' responses merely increased from 10% to 25%, with a Pearson Chi-Square (1, 40) = 1.558, $p < .212$ and Cramer's V = .197 (Veszelka, 2007).

Since it is not possible to plausibly assume that participants are unable to map the relationship contained in this thematic problem about cities and modes of transportation in a selection task but can correctly map the same relationship at 100% in an inference production task, the most plausible explanation of the lack of facilitation of 'all' responses when a response list is used is that the 'all' responses are simply more avidly avoided than the 'any' responses. That is, the selection task suggests more strongly to the participants that they cannot select 'all' cards than that they cannot select 'any' of the cards.

Both in the cases of 'any' and 'all', since participants do not find a better solution than the avoided biconditional response, they finally select those instances that are at least named in the conditional statement, the P and Q values. This non-logical 'inability to decenter from the rule' (Legrenzi, 1970; Wason, 1970), which was lately and independently redis-covered as a 'matching response' (Johnson-Laird & Wason, 1970) or 'matching bias' (Evans, 1972), has been intensively studied for several decades. It was handled as a very reliable experimental result, interpreted to show, for example, a heuristic (Evans, 1989; Evans & Over, 2004) or initial phase (Johnson-Laird & Byrne, 1991) in human reasoning.

The P and Q preference in the abstract selection task was also assumed to be a sign of heuristic thinking processes because participants were una-ble to explain this response when they were asked to do so. However, in my experiment on the thematic, ball-light selection task (Veszelka, 2007), where the 'any' response was facilitated with the response list, I also asked participants in an unpublished second phase of the experiment to explain their responses. Whereas the 60% of participants giving the 'any' response generally gave plausible equivalent explanations, the 40% still preferring the P and Q values were unable to explain their answers. They came forth with inconsistent, fragmented explanations or simply repeated parts of the task instruction, just as previously observed in the abstract selection task (see, for example, Wason, 1969).

Since the thematic, equivalent ball-light problem is assumed in the field to be easily understood, and we also have no reason to assume the opposite, all of this suggests that the P and Q preference, along with the inability of the participants to explain this preference, is only an experimental artefact specifically linked to selection tasks. Naturally, if participants reject the correct answer and are unable to find another, they cannot be expected to give a plausible explanation of their final, ad-hoc selections.

Although Evans and his colleagues also connect matching bias to abstract truth table tasks (see Evans, Clibbens & Rood, 1996; Evans & Over, 2004), it was seen earlier in this section, and will be seen in greater detail in Section 5.5, that an alternative interpretation is also possible that has the prospect of preserving the logical interpretation in these tasks.

The avoidance of the four-card selection in the selection task also explains that various manipulations, such as varying the affirmed and negated instances in the tested conditional statement, with which matching bias is assumed to be evidenced in its full effect (see Evans & Lynch, 1973; Evans, 1998; Stahl, Klauer & Erdfelder, 2008); removing or adding a card or cards (Roth, 1979; Wason & Green, 1984; Hardman, 1998; Klauer, Stahl & Erdfelder, 2007); or varying the relative set sizes to which the specific instances refer (Kirby, 1994; Yama, 2001; Nickerson & Butler, 2008) have influence on the selections. Participants do make decisions after avoiding the selection of all cards, which, as Evans and Ball (2010) observe, has regularities, but these regularities are independent of their basic interpretation of the conditional statement, and hence, are of limited importance in the study of human reasoning.

The possible biconditional interpretation of the conditional statement has always been around in the literature, but it was heavily questioned on the basis of abstract task results. However, this attitude could emerge only as a by-product of a biased experimental investigation.

On one hand, it ensued from the lack of systematic testing—for example, as shown in Table 2, until 2007, only half of the experimental results were available on the main types of tasks and negatives, and even after 2007, as far as I know, the complete results were available only in my paper, published in Hungarian. The theories in the field, as it will be shown through a few examples in this book as well, still heavily rely on these deficient experimental results. In addition, they mostly simply neglect those few experimental data that were already available for them in the field and that already showed a high proportion of equivalent responses.

On the other hand, for several decades, the literature mainly focused on the selection task. It had the most surprising result, so it was handled as a paradigmatic task for the field. However, as seen above, after running some long-missing experiments, the picture radically changes. The main experimental tasks altogether support the basic biconditional approach. This is true even for the selection task, as the seemingly illogical P and Q responses arise precisely because of the avoided, underlying equivalent response.

3.2 'EASY-TO-RESOLVE' THEMATIC SELECTION TASKS

One half of the updated classical interpretation of the conditional statement, the basic equivalent interpretation, can therefore not only be maintained, but in most cases, is even evidenced by the main reasoning experimental materials of cognitive psychology. Another empirical obstacle to this approach relates to triggering the P and not-Q answer—the traditionally expected response in logic. In the psychological literature, the elicitation of this 'correct' answer has so far been studied almost exclusively with selection tasks. In so-called thematic selection tasks, where the conditional statement is supported by an additional, thematic context, researchers obtained the allegedly correct P and not-Q response several decades ago.

The most cited task of this type is the drinking-age task of Griggs and Cox (1982), in which participants have to imagine that they are on-duty police officers who must check whether everyone observes the rule that 'If a person is drinking beer, then the person must be over 19 years of age'. 'Drinking a beer', 'drinking a cola', '22 years of age' and '16 years of age' appear on the cards. About 75% of participants select the 'drinking a beer' and '16 years of age' cards in this task—that is, the P and not-Q cards.

It is assumed in the literature that this task has the same logical structure as the abstract selection task. As a consequence, and also in line with the historical reasons illustrated in the Introduction and in Section 2.3, it is maintained that this sharp difference in the results ensues from non-logical effects. For example, these include pragmatic reasoning schemas (Cheng & Holyoak, 1985), relevance (Sperber, Cara & Girotto, 1995), deontic context (Oaksford & Chater, 1998; Stenning & van Lambalgen, 2008), cheater detection (Cosmides, 1989), precautions (Manktelow & Over, 1990) or benefits and costs (Evans & Over, 2004).

In order to advocate the updated scholastic interpretation as a possible alternative to explain everyday conditional reasoning, it is important to address these results on one hand and to interpret these non-logical explanations on the other hand.

It is clear from the very start that these explanations are not normatively valid because in the Greco-Roman or scholastic logic, or in propositional logic, where the abstraction itself has been defined, such components were clearly not present. The melting snow discussed in Section 2.1, for example, has nothing to do with deontic context or cheater detection.

Consequently, such components cannot be responsible for the relationship that was distilled out when it was embedded into an 'if-then' statement. The correct interpretation must be able to explain both of these phenomena.

Accordingly, it can be observed that there is a wedging of information in the easy-to-resolve selection tasks, which mainly correspond to the effect of alternative antecedents in the updated scholastic interpretation. In the above task, everyone knows that people over 19 years of age can drink both alcohol and soft drinks, although this is not explicitly communicated in the task instruction.

This also means that the logical structure of the abstract and the easy-to-resolve thematic selection tasks are different. One of the experiments of Hoch and Tschirgi (1983, p. 203) can be seen as a means to test the effect of this additional information. They used an abstract selection task, with the appropriate substitutions, with the statement that 'Cards with a P on the front may only have Q on the back, but cards with not-P on the front may have either Q or not-Q on the back'. This cue facilitation produced correct results 56% of the time in the authors' experiment. However, in the replication of the experimental condition (Hoch & Tschirgi, 1985), the rate was only 36% in the usual experimental population. Further, participants with knowledge of logic were not filtered out; this could evidently improve the result, since logically literate participants could, of course, be aware of the response that was expected of them.

With the usual experimental population having no knowledge of logic, and with the usual task layout, only a modest improvement was achieved with this type of facilitation (Platt & Griggs, 1993). This task has so far been tested only in the selection task. In the following experiment, I re-tested this task in the selection and inference production tasks to see if the lack of correct performance is linked to a general failure of understanding the conditional relation embedded in this problem, or if it is linked once again specifically to the selection task.

3.3 EXPERIMENT 1 – TESTING HOCH AND TSCHIRGI'S CUE FACILITATION

3.3.1 Participants

Twenty-one students from the Eötvös Loránd University, Pedagogical and Psychological Faculty, Hungary, participated in the experiment within the framework of an introductory psychology course. None of them had any training in logic, nor were any of them familiar with tasks of this type.

3.3.2 Materials

This experiment investigated the cue-facilitated problem of Hoch and Tschirgi (1983, 1985) in the selection task and in the inference production task. In the conditional statement, instead of mentioning specific letters and numbers, the initial vowel-consonant and odd-even phrasing of Wason (1966, 1968) was used.

The selection task was stated as follows:

> Four cards are lying in front of you. On one side of the cards, there is a letter; on the other side, there is a number. Suppose that if on one of the sides, there is a vowel, then there must be an even number on the other side, but if there is a consonant on one of the sides, then both an odd and an even number can figure on the other side.

Which card or cards must be turned over in order to decide if this is true?

The cards had the following values, respectively:

A   C   4   3

The inference production task was stated as follows:

> Imagine a pack of cards. On one side of the cards, there is a letter; on the other side, there is a number. Suppose that if on one of the sides, there is a consonant, then there must be an even number on the other side, but if there is a vowel on one of the sides, then both an odd and an even number can figure on the other side. What follows? Continue the following sentences:
>
> There is a letter G on one of the sides; therefore:
>
> There is a letter E on one of the sides; therefore:
>
> There is a number 5 on one of the sides; therefore:
>
> There is a number 2 on one of the sides; therefore:

Apart from the specific letters and numbers presented on the cards and from the insertion of the phrase 'Imagine a pack of cards' in the instruction of the inference production task for interpretive reasons, the difference between the two tasks was merely the placement of the vowel and the consonant in the task; that is, in the selection task, the vowel was to co-occur with the even number and a consonant could co-occur with both an even and an odd number, whereas in the inference production task, the situation was just the opposite.

3.3.3   Procedure

All participants solved both tasks. Half of them resolved the selection task first, and half of them resolved the inference production task first. Therefore, two groups were created. Five minutes were allowed to solve the tasks. The tasks were administered in the Hungarian language.

3.3.4   Results

Table 4. The results of the abstract 'cue-facilitated' problem of Experiment 1 in the selection and inference production tasks

Responses	Selection task		Inference production task	
	S-I*	I-S†	S-I*	I-S†
P	-	3	1	1
P, Q	1	-	-	-
P, Not-P	1	-	-	-
P, Not-Q	2	1	7	9
P, Not-P, Q	3	1	-	-
P, Q, Not-Q	2	2	1	-
Q, Not-Q	-	1	-	-
Not-P, Q	-	1	-	-
All	1	1	-	-
None of them	-	-	-	-
No answer	-	1	1	1
N	10	11	10	11

*S-I: First, the selection task, and then inference production task
†I-S: First, the inference production task, and then selection task

Table 4 displays every response that occurred at least once in the experiment. In order to compare the results of the two tasks more effectively, the results of the inference production task are also expressed via the logical instances. The modus ponens is recorded as 'P' because the minor premise of this inference is P; the denial of the antecedent is recorded as 'not-P' because this is its minor premise, and so forth. An inference was recorded as endorsed when a participant actually endorsed that inference. It was not accepted as a valid inference when a participant indicated a logically impermissible conclusion, such as inferring from not-Q that both P and not-P hold, or when he or she said regarding an inference that it is 'probable'.

As shown in Table 4, the answers to the selection task were very miscellaneous and difficult to interpret, with merely 14% providing correct answers overall, while for the same problem in the inference production task, when the task was solved before the selection task, the correct answer rate reached 82%. Taken together, of the results from both groups, the rate of correct responses was still 76% in the inference production task, which, compared to the 14% of the selection task, was, of course, a significant difference (Pearson Chi-Square $(1, 42) = 16.243, p < .0001$, Cramer's V = .622).

These results indicate that the inference production task already confirms the assumption outlined earlier. The difference was particularly interesting because all participants resolved both tasks. No significant difference in the results of the selection task was observed with regard to whether the participants solved the inference production task first or only after the selection task (Pearson Chi-Square $(1, 21) = .509, p < .476$, Cramer's V = .156). That is, when the inference production task was performed first, the high rate of correct answers (82%) had no transfer at all to the selection task; the selection task produced correct selections in only 9% of responses. This suggests that the selection task itself is responsible for the lack of correct responses, not the inability of the participants to map the relation contained in the conditional statement.

In the selection task, once again, people perhaps want to test the complete relationship by determining, for instance, that both P and not-P can figure on the card with a Q on its other side. This would again require turning over all four cards, and as such, the distorting effect mentioned in Section 3.1 in the case of the standard abstract selection task could reappear. Maybe this intention to check the complete relationship was blocked by Platt and Griggs (1993) when using Hoch and Tschirgi's extended conditional statement; by asking participants card by card if they want to turn over the given cards, and also by asking them to give explanations for their decisions, they managed to evoke 67-81% P and not-Q responses in this abstract selection task.

Similarly, it can be observed that, contrary to the standard facilitation attempt of Hoch and Tschirgi (1983), in the easy-to-resolve drinking-age selection task that was discussed in Section 3.2, the relationship that people over 19 years can also drink cola is from outside of the task and is not included in the investigated conditional statement. As a result, it must not be part of the examination. For this reason, in the following experiment, I constructed an abstract selection task that was analogous even in this respect to the drinking-age selection task.

3.4   EXPERIMENT 2 – THE 'EASY TO RESOLVE' ABSTRACT SELECTION TASK

3.4.1   Participants

Forty-three students from the Eötvös Loránd University, Pedagogical and Psychological Faculty, Hungary, participated in the experiment within the framework of an introductory psychology course. None of them had any training in logic, nor were any of them familiar with tasks of this type.

3.4.2   Materials

An abstract selection task was designed in which the alternative 'or R' antecedent was embedded into the task from general background knowledge, without being explicitly named in the investigated conditional statement. This 'facilitated' abstract task was stated as follows:

> Imagine that four cards are lying in front of you on the table. On one side of the card, there is either the number 4 or the number 6; on the other side, there is either 'divisible by two' or 'divisible by three'. Your task is to check whether each of the four cards on the table conforms with the reality, namely, with the rule that:
>
> If the number is 4, then it is divisible by only two.
>
> Which card or cards would you turn over to check this?
>
> The cards had the following values: '4', '6', 'divisible by two' and 'divisible by three', respectively.

In the control task, I replaced '6' with '3' in the instruction and on the second card. In order to ensure better text comprehension, I also removed the word 'only' from the 'if-then' statement. According to my interpretation, therefore, the two tasks evoke two different relationships, as shown in Figure 1.

With number 6, the task produces the conditional inference pattern, and with number 3, the biconditional pattern. The lines above the cards were not displayed on the experimental material.

| 4 | 6 | Divisible by two | Divisible by three |

| 4 | 3 | Divisible by two | Divisible by three |

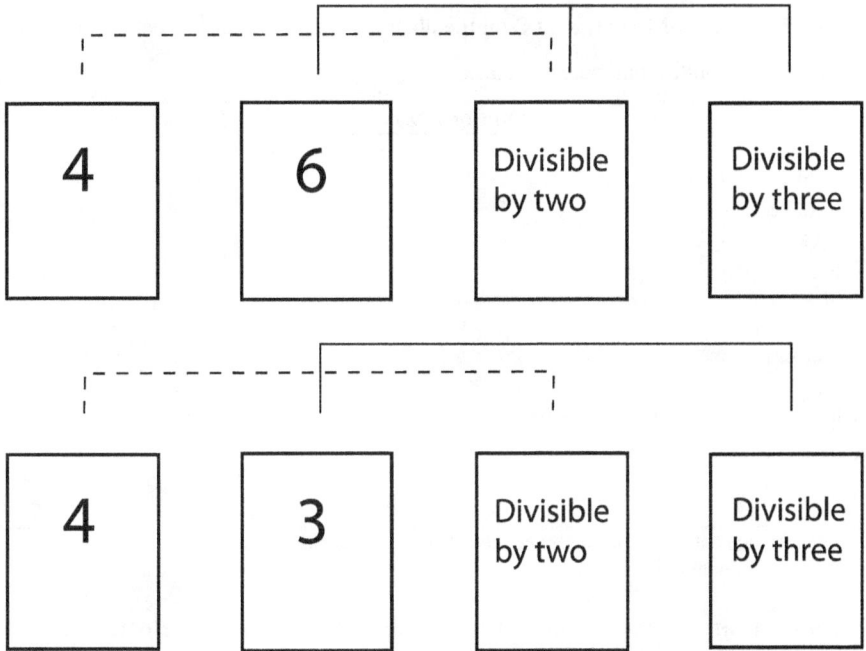

Figure 1. Cards and evoked relations in the experiment on the easy-to-resolve abstract selection task

3.4.3   Procedure

Everyone resolved only one task; there were two groups. Five minutes were allowed to resolve the task. The experiment was conducted in Hungarian.

3.4.4   Results

As shown in Table 5, sharp differences occurred in the results of the two tasks. In the abstract selection task with the 'P or R then Q' relationship, the predominant answer was the joint selection of the P and not-Q cards

Table 5. Results of Experiment 2 on the abstract 'biconditional' selection task and the abstract 'conditional' selection task

	Biconditional task	Conditional task
P	-	4
P, Not-P	-	1
P, Not-Q*	1	9
P, Q	9	1
Not-P, Not-Q	-	1
Not-P, Q	-	1
Q	-	2
Q, Not-Q	2	-
Not-Q	1	-
All†	8	2
No answer	-	1
N	21	22

*The inference pattern traditionally equated with the conditional statement
†The biconditional inference pattern

(41%), the traditional P and Q response (4.5%) and the selection of all cards (9%), which could be connected to the biconditional relation, not having reached 14% altogether.

In contrast, in the biconditional task, the frequency of the 'P and not-Q' response was a mere 5%, whereas the rate of the 'P and Q' selection was 43%, and that of the 'all' was 38%. The difference among these three response patterns is obvious, with a Pearson Chi-Square $(3, 43) = 20.157$, $p < .0002$ and Cramer's V = .685, and because of the minimal differences between the tasks, it explains itself. With an alternative antecedent embedded into the abstract selection task 'from outside', it can be transformed into a task that has the traditionally expected conditional response as the most characteristic solution.

Although it would be difficult to locate, for example, Cosmides's (1989) cheater detection in this easy-to-resolve abstract selection task, the task can be seen as a deontic task in the sense that the rule itself cannot be rejected on the basis of what appears on the cards; only violating instances can be found, much as in thematic tasks prescribing a given behaviour to follow (see, for instance, Oaksford & Chater, 1994; Evans & Over, 2004; Stenning & van Lambalgen, 2008). Still, the relatively good solution to this task cannot be explained by this deontic aspect. If we follow this interpretation, the control biconditional abstract task was also deontic, yet still, it did not evoke the traditionally prescribed response.

3.5 EXPERIMENT 3 – FURTHER FACILITATION ATTEMPT

However, at a different university, where participants were given twice as much time to resolve the tasks, I failed to reproduce the above results to the same degree.

A colleague raised the point that the IQ scores for the two universities have a similar difference; hence, IQ could possibly also play a role in the way the tasks are resolved. For this reason, with Anikó Kecse Nagy, we tested the tasks in the summer camp of Mensa HungarIQa. This organization collects Hungarians older than 17 years of age who have obtained a score on the Raven's Advanced Progressive Matrices IQ test higher than 98% of the general Hungarian population.

3.5.1 Participants

Forty members of the Hungarian Mensa group participated in the experiment in the frame of the summer camp of the organisation.

3.5.2   Materials

The experimental material was identical with the two tasks of Experiment 2.

3.5.3   Procedure

Participants were voluntary applicants who resolved the task in a room. Five minutes were allowed for the task. In order not to discriminate against those who had prior knowledge in logic and in an attempt not to overcomplicate the administration of the experiment, anyone was allowed to resolve the task; participants merely had to indicate on the worksheet whether they had preliminary knowledge of logic or not.

3.5.4   Results

Table 6. Results of Experiment 3 on the 'biconditional' abstract selection task and the 'conditional' abstract selection task

	Biconditional task		Conditional task	
	Result	Knowl. in L[‡]	Result	Knowl. in L[‡]
P	3	/1/	-	-
P, Q	2	/1/	2	-
P, Not-Q[*]	6	/4/	11	/6/
P, Q, Not-Q	1	-	-	-
Q	-	-	1	-
Q, Not-Q	1	/1/	-	-
Not-Q	-	-	2	/1/
All[†]	5	/4/	-	-
None of them	1	-	-	-
No solution	1	/1/	-	-
N	20	/12/	16	/7/

[*]The inference pattern traditionally equated with the conditional statement
[†]The biconditional inference pattern
[‡]Number of participants with knowledge in logic

The results are shown in Table 6. Four participants were excluded from the data because they were already familiar with the task. They were all from the 'conditional' group, with knowledge of logic, and they all selected the

P and not-Q cards. In total, the results were 69% vs. 30% 'P and not-Q' answers, with Pearson Chi-Square $(1, 36) = 5.355$, $p < .021$ and Cramer's $V = .386$ for the conditional task versus the biconditional task. The difference among the 'all' biconditional answers was also significant in the opposite direction (0% vs. 25%), with Pearson Chi-Square $(1, 36) = 4.645$, $p < .031$ and Cramer's $V = .359$. Deconstructing the results further, 55% of the participants with no knowledge of logic (five out of nine subjects) gave the 'P and not-Q' answer to the conditional task, while 25% of them gave the same answer to the biconditional task. Even participants with knowledge of logic produced significantly more P and not-Q answers to the conditional task (86% vs. 33%), with Pearson Chi-Square $(1, 19) = 4.866$, $p < .027$ and Cramer's $V = .506$, and more 'all' responses to the biconditional task (0 vs. 33%), with Pearson Chi-Square $(1, 19) = 2.956$, $p < .086$ and Cramer's $V = .394$.

The experiment did not confirm the effect of IQ on the rate of correct solutions. The increase in the rate of correct responses of logically untrained participants compared to the previous experiment did not reach significance. Still, the 55% rate of correct solutions of the Mensa members unfamiliar with logic is already considerably high. Although it is below the usual 70–75% rate of easy-to-resolve thematic selection tasks, Fiddick and Erlich (2010, Exp. 1) also received P and not-Q selections in only 54% of cases when the participants were explicitly instructed to search for the falsifying co-occurrence of P and not-Q in the abstract selection task. That is, when they were explicitly given the solution, they only had to tick the corresponding cards. It is therefore conceivable that this is the maximum rate of success one could reasonably expect from this task.

Whereas we have therefore an easy-to-resolve abstract selection task and hence an empirically verified explanation for the lack of traditional conditional responses in the traditional abstract selection task, there are two differences between the traditional abstract selection tasks and the tasks tested in Experiments 2 and 3. The text of the tasks in Experiments 2 and 3 referred to a rule that 'conforms with the reality', and the easy-to-resolve abstract selection task had the word 'only' in the tested conditional statement. To make the results perfectly comparable to each other, in the following experiment, I have tested the effect of these additional components.

3.6   EXPERIMENT 4 – ANCILLARY COMPONENTS

3.6.1   Participants

One hundred twenty-five students from the Eötvös Loránd University, Pedagogical and Psychological Faculty, Hungary, participated in the experiment within the framework of an introductory psychology course. None of them had any training in logic, nor were any of them familiar with tasks of this type. Participants were requested to indicate on the answer sheets if they happened to know the Wason selection task. Four participants reported being familiar with this, so their results were subsequently excluded from the data.

3.6.2   Materials

In addition to retesting the tasks used in Experiments 2 and 3 for control purposes, the easy-to-resolve abstract selection task was also tested in an experimental condition in which the word 'only' was removed from the conditional statement, and also in a condition in which both 'only' and 'conforms with the reality' were removed.

The former condition made the easy-to-resolve abstract selection task take on exactly the same form as the abstract biconditional selection task of Experiments 2 and 3. In this condition, the only difference between these tasks was whether '6' or '3' figured on the second card and was mentioned in the task instruction.

The latter condition, on the other hand, where both 'only' and 'conforms with the reality' were removed, made the tested abstract selection task, from an experimental point of view, completely identical to the usual abstract selection tasks used in the field.

In addition, the abstract biconditional selection task of Experiments 2 and 3 was also tested in a condition where the word 'only' was added to its conditional statement. This made the abstract conditional selection task of Experiments 2 and 3 and this abstract biconditional selection task take on the same form, again with the mere difference of whether '6' or '3' was used on the second card and in the task instruction. This way, I created two task variants in which only the embedded logical relations were different between the conditional and the biconditional task.

3.6.3   Procedure

The experiment ran under the same conditions as Experiment 2, except that the experiment was performed one year later.

3.6.4   Results

As shown in Table 7, this experiment also confirmed the relatively good performance on the easy-to-resolve selection task of Experiments 2 and 3 (out of 22 participants, 41% gave this answer). Removing the 'only' re-

Table 7. The results of Experiment 4 on the ancillary components of the 'easy to resolve' abstract selection task

	Control biconditional	Biconditional with 'only'	Conditional without 'reality' and 'only'	Conditional without 'only'	Control conditional
P	3	1	2	4	1
Q	5	3	2	2	2
P, Q	7	7	10	9	2
All	3	7	–	1	1
P & Not-Q	3	3	–	1	1
P, Q, Not-Q	2	4	3	5	9
Not-P	1	–	–	–	2
Not-P & Q	–	1	1	–	1
Not-P & Not-Q	2	–	2	–	2
Not-Q	–	2	2	1	1
None	2	1	1	–	–
No answer	–	1	5	–	–
Any	–	–	1	–	–
N	25	25	27	22	22

duced the correct results to 23%, which shows a statistically tendentious difference, with Pearson Chi-Square $(1, 44) = 3.536$, $p < .06$ and Cramer's $V = .283$. Removing both 'only' and 'conforms with the reality' reduced the correct results even further, to 11%, which is already a statistically significant difference compared to the standard wording of the easy-to-resolve abstract selection task of Experiments 2 and 3 (Pearson Chi-Square $(1, 49) = 8.983$, $p < .003$, Cramer's $V = .428$).

It is clear, therefore, that these components are important factors in evoking the expected conditional responses. However, if we add the 'only' component to the conditional statement of the biconditional selection task tested in Experiments 2 and 3 (the 'conforms with the reality' component was already present in the task instruction), there is no statistically detectable increase in the rate of conditional selections (8% vs. 16%, which is 2 out of 25 vs. 4 out of 25 participants), with Pearson Chi-Square $(1, 50) = .758$, $p < .384$ and Cramer's $V = .123$. Therefore, even though the wording of the easy-to-resolve abstract selection task reported in this book greatly assists in evoking the correct conditional inferences, likely making the task and the embedded relationship easier to understand, the actual relationship embedded in the task still plays a crucial role in the responses.

The difference between the conditional and the biconditional task in terms of the 'P and not-Q' selections can remain high even when the wording of the tasks is exactly the same. When both tasks include the word 'only' in the conditional statement, a significant difference exists between the tasks in terms of the evoked 'P and not-Q' selections (41% vs. 16%), with Pearson Chi-Square $(1, 47) = 4.382$, $p < .036$ and Cramer's $V = .305$. However, when none of the tasks include the word 'only', no statistically detectable difference exists in the 'P and not-Q' selections (23% vs. 8%), with Pearson Chi-Square $(1, 47) = 2.002$, $p < .157$ and Cramer's $V = .206$.

Similarly, in case of the 'all' responses, no significant differences exist, but remember that the 'all' response is an avoided response.

3.7   EXPERIMENT 5 – FURTHER CONTROL TESTS

Since we have already seen in Section 3.1 how misleading conclusions can be reached if the experimental tasks are not tested systematically, in this additional experiment, I tested the 'biconditional' and 'conditional' abstract problems of Experiment 4 in truth table, simple inference and inference production tasks.

To make the results easily comparable, I ran this experiment so that both problems included the word 'only' in their conditional statements and the phrase 'conforms with the reality' task instruction component. That is, I principally tested two problem variants that were already tested in the selection task in Experiment 4. The question was whether the equivalent and conditional answers would also appear in the three other main tasks, and if so, in what proportion.

In addition, I also wanted to run some tests on how problems traditionally accepted as equivalent or conditional problems perform in these additional tasks. The thematic ball-light problem, which is traditionally accepted in the field as an equivalent problem, has only been tested in truth table tasks in the literature, but we have already discussed in Section 3.1 how this problem performs in selection tasks and in inference production tasks. In case of this problem, therefore, only the result of the traditional simple inference task is missing.

On the other hand, in the case of the drinking-age problem of Griggs and Cox (1982), which is commonly accepted in the literature as an 'easy to resolve' conditional problem, results are available only in the selection task. Because of the already limited number of experimental participants, however, I could choose only two experimental conditions out of these four, and I decided to test the drinking-age problem in truth table and inference production tasks. The reason for selecting these tasks was that with abstract problems, the truth table task produces maybe the most problematic results (not taking into account, of course, the selection task that we have already discussed in this book in detail), and the inference production task the most favourable results.

3.7.1 Participants

One hundred three students from the Eötvös Loránd University, Pedagogical and Psychological Faculty, Hungary, participated in the experiment within the framework of an introductory psychology course. None of them had any training in logic, nor were any of them familiar with tasks of this type.

3.7.2 Materials

The texts of the abstract equivalent and conditional problems were exactly the same, except that in the equivalent problem, the number '3' was present, and in the conditional problem, the number '6' was present. The task variants in this experiment were based on those tasks of Experiment 4 that contained the word 'only' in their conditional statements. The texts of the equivalent tasks can be seen below. Simply replacing the number '3' with '6' in these tasks immediately reproduces the text of the conditional tasks.

The text of the abstract equivalent inference production task was as follows:

Imagine cards that can have only the numbers 3 or 4 on one of their sides, and the other side of them can only say whether the given number is divisible by two or three. Suppose that the cards were prepared so that they would display the following real rule:

If the number is 4, then it is divisible by only two.

What follows? Continue the following sentences:

The number is the 4; therefore:

The number is the 3; therefore:

The number is 'divisible by two'; therefore:

The number is 'divisible by three'; therefore:

The equivalent simple inference task was exactly the same as the equivalent inference production task, with the mere difference that after the tested conditional statement, the task continued as follows:

Please underline if the following inferences are true, false or irrelevant in light of the rule above:

The number is '4'; therefore, it is divisible by two.

The number is '4'; therefore, it is divisible by three.

The number is '3'; therefore, it is divisible by two.

The number is '3' therefore, it is divisible by three.

The number is divisible by two; therefore, it is the number '4'.

The number is divisible by two; therefore, it is the number '3'.

The number is divisible by three; therefore, it is the number '4'.

The number is divisible by three; therefore, it is the number '3'.

All these inferences were followed one by one by the following three response options:

True inference   False inference   Irrelevant inference

The text of the equivalent truth table task was also different from the two tasks above only after the conditional statement. This different part was stated as follows:

Please underline in the case of the number-divider pairs below if they verify or falsify the rule, or if they are irrelevant:

'Number 4' and 'divisible by two':

'Number 4' and 'divisible by three':

'Number 3' and 'divisible by two':

'Number 3' and 'divisible by three':

All these number-divider pairs were followed one by one by the following three response options:

Verifies the rule   Falsifies the rule   Irrelevant with regard to the rule

The drinking-age problem was presented in the inference production task as follows (Note: The text reflects that in Hungary, the age limit for drinking alcohol is 18 years):

Imagine that you are a police officer on duty in a bar and have to check that everyone observes the following rule:

If someone is drinking alcohol, he or she must be over 18 years of age.

What follows? Continue the following sentences:

A person is drinking alcohol; therefore:

A person doesn't drink alcohol; therefore:

A person is older than 18 years; therefore:

A person is younger than 18 years; therefore:

In the drinking-age truth table task, the text of the task differed only after the conditional statement. This part of the task was stated as follows:

Please underline in the case of the people below if they follow the rule, violate the rule or their consumption is irrelevant with regard to the rule:

'Drinks alcohol' and is 'older than 18 years'

''Drinks alcohol' and is 'younger than 18 years'

'Doesn't drink alcohol' and is 'older than 18 years'

'Doesn't drink alcohol' and is 'younger than 18 years'

All these co-occurrences were followed one by one by the following three response options:

Verifies the rule   Falsifies the rule   Irrelevant with regard to the rule

3.7.3   Procedure

The experiment was run under the same conditions as Experiment 4, but during the next semester.

3.7.4   Results

Table 8. The rates of correct equivalent/conditional solutions in Experiment 5 received via the main tasks of the field other than the selection task on the abstract 'conditional' and 'biconditional' problems tested in this book, and on the thematic drinking-age problem

	Truth table task	Simple inference task	Inference production task
Abstract equivalent problem	3 out of 12 (25%)	4 out of 12 (33%)	12 out of 12 (100%)
Abstract conditional problem	3 out of 13 (23%)	0 or 11 out of 14 (0% or 79%)[*]	10 out of 14 (71%)
Drinking-age problem	1 out of 14 (7%)	not tested	9 out of 12 (75%)

[*]The exact match with the dictates of traditional logic is 0%, but there is good reason to believe the correct response rate was, in fact, much higher. More about this in the main text.

The overall results are shown in Table 8. It can be seen that the logically correct solution appeared only in the inference production task in a high proportion for all three problems. In the simple inference task, the abstract problems had a much more ambiguous result (and the drinking-age problem was not tested), whereas in the truth table task, all three problems yielded poor results.

The merely 7% correct response rate for the drinking-age problem in the truth table task is particularly surprising, as this problem is believed to be generally 'easy to resolve'. As seen in Section 3.2, there are many non-logical explanations for the high rate of correct solutions for this drinking-age problem. All these non-logical explanations lose their explanatory power as soon as the problem is tested in the truth table task instead of the selection task. Obviously, we cannot assume that the cheater detection that Cosmides (1989) and her co-workers assume as the explanation of the good performance on the drinking-age problem is evolutionarily encoded in us only in the selection task, but not so in the truth table task. We cannot say either that deontic logic, as assumed, for example, by Stenning and van Lambalgen (2008), is operational only in the selection task but not so in the truth table task.

To maintain their approach, even these researchers have to assume that the truth table task distorts the results. For this reason, the main problem with this result is basically that on the basis of this truth table task, researchers have explained for decades how people infer on the abstract conditional statement, and hence, on the conditional statement in general.

In Evans and Over's (2004) approach, the truth table tasks still play an important role. The authors assume on the basis of these tasks that the everyday interpretation of the conditional statement, at least, as they say, in the case of abstract problems, could be the defective truth table of Kneale and Kneale (1962), which was lately and independently rediscovered by Wason (1966) as well. This defective truth table has already been discussed in Section 3.1 and in Footnote 2. The authors currently link this defective truth table to the Ramsey test, and ultimately, to Edgington's (2003) suppositional theory, where people do not infer from the negated antecedents.

However, from an experimental point of view, Evans and Over's (2004) approach can be questioned for several reasons. It can be questioned by the results of the abstract truth table tasks with dichotomous negatives, where people clearly infer in case of the negated antecedents (see Tables 2 & 3). It can also be questioned by the results of the abstract inference production tasks in general (see Table 3), where people obviously infer from the negated antecedents. Finally, it can now also be questioned by this result of the drinking age truth table task, since, according to the interpretation of the authors, this non abstract problem has to be 'easy to resolve'.

Table 9. The frequencies of the evaluation of the truth table cases in the abstract equivalent problem, the abstract conditional problem and the drinking-age problem in the truth table task of Experiment 5

	TT	TF	FT	FF
Abstract equivalent task				
True	11 (92%)	-	-	5 (42%)
False	1 (8%)	11 (92%)	4 (33%)	1 (8%)
Irrelevant	-	1 (8%)	8 (67%)	6 (50%)
Abstract conditional task				
True	11 (85%)	-	4 (31%)	5 (39%)
False	-	10 (77%)	4 (31%)	2 (15%)
Irrelevant	2 (15%)	3 (23%)	5 (38%)	6 (46%)
Drinking-age task				
True	12 (86%)	-	1 (7%)	9 (64%)
False	-	14 (100%)	-	-
Irrelevant	2 (14%)	-	13 (93%)	5 (36%)

Since the truth table task performed so poorly even with a thematic, 'easy to resolve' conditional problem, it is not so problematic, from the point of view of logic, that it does not perform well with abstract problems, either. This is particularly so because the abstract 'conditional' and 'equivalent' problems of this experiment and the drinking-age problem produced very similar results overall in this truth table task, as shown in Table 9.

Among the three problems, principally, only the FT case revealed statistically detectable differences. This could even be seen as reasonable, since, according to the traditional interpretation, the equivalent and the conditional relationship differ only in the FT case in the truth table (as shown in Table 1). However, the difference is not what is contained in the traditional truth tables. It ensues from the FT case being evaluated mostly as irrelevant in the drinking-age task.

As such, with the FT case, there is a statistically tendentious difference between the two abstract problems (Pearson Chi-Square $(1, 25) = 4.66$, $p < .097$, Cramer's V = .432), a statistically significant difference between the two conditional problems (Pearson Chi-Square $(1, 27) = 9.331$, $p < .009$, Cramer's V = .588) and finally, a statistically significant difference again between the abstract equivalent problem and the drinking-age problem

(Pearson Chi-Square $(1, 26) = 6.073$, $p < .048$, Cramer's V = .483). In addition, a statistically tendentious difference has also appeared between the two conditional problems in the TF case (Pearson Chi-Square $(1, 27) = 3.635$, $p < .057$, Cramer's V = .367).

Although the results hence suggest that the abstract equivalent task is closer to the drinking-age task than the abstract conditional task, we have no reason to assume this, so this difference might be merely accidental; further experiments may not strengthen it. It is, however, clear on the basis of the obtained results that the truth table task is rather ill-suited to differentiate between the three theoretically markedly different problems.

Another unexpected outcome of this experiment was that the abstract equivalent and conditional problems also performed poorly in the truth table task and in the simple inference task. Since, as we have just seen, the drinking-age problem also yielded wrong solutions in the truth table task, this does not necessarily represent a serious counterargument against the basic assumptions advanced in this book.

In the case of the simple inference task, for the abstract conditional problem, no correct conditional inferences appeared when utilising the traditional logical interpretation. However, 11 out of 14 persons were actually 100% correct on the MP, DA and MT inferences; they deviated only in the case of the AC inference, labelling the two corresponding inferences in the datasheet as both irrelevant (6 participants), as both false (4 participants) or as the first irrelevant and the second false (1 participant). However, both the 'irrelevant' and the 'false' evaluations can be justified. With the 'If the number is 4, then it is divisible by only two' statement, and 4 and 6 as P and not-P values, respectively, it is reasonable to label the 'AC' inference as irrelevant, since when the number is divisible by two, it can be both 6 and 4, not merely 4, and not merely 6, as it was stated in the task response options. That is, since the AC inference was not displayed with the conclusion 'both 4 and 6', participants could prefer selecting 'irrelevant' or 'false', instead of selecting 'true'. If the reader can accept this interpretation, these 11 people actually correctly mapped the conditional relationship. Once again, it's the experimental task that distorts the results.

In short, therefore, merely the abstract equivalent problem in the simple inference task produced a result which definitely seems inconsistent with the views advocated in this book. This led me to suppose that this finding is because of the word 'only' in the conditional statement, which is principally inconsistent with the equivalent relationship. Drawing, for example, the denial of the antecedent inference from the 'If P then *only* Q' statement, we can obtain that 'If not-P then *not only* Q', but this is inconsistent with the context of the equivalent abstract problem, where in the case of not-P, only not-Q can follow. In a pilot study on seven and eight students, I tested the abstract biconditional problem used in this book without the word 'only' in the truth table task and the simple inference task, respectively. This pilot study was run in a seminar of Eötvös Loránd University, Pedagogical and Psychological Faculty, Hungary, with five minutes allowed to solve the tasks. However, the results were still very miscellaneous, with only 29% and 13% correct responses, respectively.

There are, therefore, still unclear points with regard to abstract problems. The poor performance on the abstract equivalent problem used in this book in the truth table and simple inference tasks is particularly surprising because this problem is a dichotomous problem, and as we have seen in Tables 2 and 3, the standard abstract problem evokes 42-83% equivalent responses in these tasks with similar dichotomous negatives.

To determine what is responsible for the lack of equivalent responses in these tasks, I asked six people between 30 and 40 years of age to solve the abstract equivalent problem used in this book, without the word 'only' in the simple inference task used in Experiment 5, and then interviewed them about their responses. Half of them actually provided an equivalent solution, and another two of them selected at a few places the response option 'irrelevant' only because they expected a 'trick' from the task and believed that having 'irrelevant' as a response option meant that they actually had to do something with this option. I was able to very easily convince them about the equivalence inference pattern as being the correct solution. Only one person was decisive about not inferring from the negated antecedent and instead providing the 'irrelevant' responses. So, in sum, these interviews suggest that the performance on the 'equivalent' abstract tasks tested in this book can generally be reconciled with the basic equivalent interpretation advanced in this book, particularly as we have already seen substantial evidence showing that expecting such 'tricks' from the experimental tasks can distort the results.

3.8   DISCUSSION OF THE EXPERIMENTAL PART

In general, despite some unexpected data in Experiment 5, the main experimental tasks of cognitive psychology not only allow us to maintain the updated classical interpretation of the conditional statement, but many of them even directly evidence it.

On one hand, researchers such as Markovits and his colleagues (Markovits, 1985; Markovits, Venet, Janveau-Brennan, Malfait, Pion & Vadeboncoeur, 1996), Byrne and her colleagues (Byrne, 1989; Byrne et al., 1999) or Cummins, Lubart, Alksnis and Rist (1991) have already demonstrated its basic mechanism with simple inference tasks on so-called arbitrary thematic materials, where the propositions are not abstract, but their relationships to each other are arbitrary.

On the other hand, as shown in this book, the main experimental tasks with content- and context-free, abstract conditional statements also support, in general, the assumption that people basically interpret the conditional statement as an equivalent relation, and with the effect of alternative antecedents, this modifies into the relationship known as the conditional. Being abstract, or in other words, content- and context free, actually means that in these problems, the propositions are not embedded into additional background relations apart from what is explicitly stated by the conditional statement.

It was seen that when adding an alternative antecedent to the abstract conditional statement—creating a problem called, in this book, the 'easy to resolve' abstract problem—two out of the four main tasks, the inference production task and, with some interpretative help, the simple inference task, revealed high traditional conditional responses (Experiment 5), and the third main task, the selection task, showed moderately high traditional conditional responses (Experiments 2, 3, 4). Although the fourth task, the truth table task, evoked conditional answers to a very modest degree, the same happened in this task with the drinking-age problem of Griggs and Cox (1982), which is widely accepted in the field as evoking conditional responses and as 'easy to resolve'. Consequently, the lack of the conditional responses to these two problems in the truth table task suggests a possible distorting effect of the task rather than a general failure of the participants to grasp the conditional relationship embedded in these problems.

When transforming the conditional relationship in the 'easy to resolve' abstract problem into an equivalent relationship by merely replacing a number, this 'equivalent' abstract problem evoked equivalent responses 100% of the time in the inference production task (Experiment 5). In the other three main tasks, even though the rates of conditional responses were greatly reduced, the correct equivalent responses were given only 12-38% of the time (Experiments 2, 3, 4, 5). This is somewhat in contrast with what was found with the traditional abstract problem, which evoked equivalent responses 42-83% of the time in the simple inference and truth table tasks with similar dichotomous negatives (as shown in Tables 2 & 3).

In the selection task, the lack of equivalent responses can be explained by the avoidance of the selection of 'all' cards, which, as discussed, was also demonstrated on a thematic, definitely biconditional problem, and a similar effect was also demonstrated on the biconditional ball-light problem having the 'any' solution as its correct response (see Section 3.1).

However, the discrepancy in the truth table task and in the simple inference task between the traditional abstract problem and the 'equivalent' abstract problem used in this book requires further testing. This question can be best investigated by explicitly interviewing participants about their responses. A pilot interview of six persons solving the abstract 'equivalent' simple inference task used in Experiment 5 suggests that the results of these abstract 'equivalent' problems can also easily be reconciled with the updated scholastic interpretation of the conditional statement. But even if this were not so, altogether, the predominant response to those abstract problems discussed in this book that have no alternative antecedents in their conditional statements is still the equivalent inference pattern.

In sum, the main reasoning tasks of cognitive psychology provide fairly good experimental support for the approach advanced in this book. Some of the tasks distort the results, but these effects can be taken into account or studied further, and their results can then be effectively used to demonstrate everyday logical inferences in an empirical way.

It must be noted that in addition to the experimental tasks and problems discussed here, there are a great number of additional, less central experimental tasks and problems in the field. Evans, one of the predominant and most established researchers in the field since its inception, has bemoaned several times the fragmented nature of the literature (see Evans, 1991, 1995) and the inconsistent experimental results (Evans & Over, 2004). Naturally, if the whole of the literature, being led, among others, by Evans, has been unable to yield consistent and systematic results or to address these problems, then the resolution to this dilemma cannot be expected from this single book, either. Quite simply, the number of experimental participants is limited, and the book could become convoluted by testing and questioning relatively insignificant experimental findings, one after the other, just to show, for instance, why they are not reliable. For this reason, I could only aim to make consistent at least the results of the most important experimental tasks, and since many results are already missing even here, this is in itself a big step towards understanding how people actually draw inferences from the conditional statement.

Although there are still some puzzling data, the obtained results can be quite effectively reconciled with each other and with what we have concluded in Section 2 about the traditional abstraction of the conditional statement. Overall, the results support that in everyday life, the conditional statement is basically interpreted as an equivalent relation, and this relation develops into the traditional conditional relationship when an alternative antecedent is added.

This basic equivalent relationship is a logical and easily identifiable inference pattern. It has long been known by anyone with at least a minimal knowledge of logic. However, though it is known, it may not be well understood. It is generally assumed to be a fallacy, but it is, in fact, an inference pattern that can be defended even as a logically correct response if we take into account how the conditional statement was actually abstracted in logic.

Of course, if we do not take this into account, but posit, irrespectively of the historical facts, that this is an axiom, then naturally, it cannot be refuted. But even then, or even if the reader finds the historical considerations in this book misleading, the experiments presented in this experimental section still show that the basic equivalent relationship, as well as the mechanism of how it expands as a result of additional propositions, could be a good starting point to describe everyday thinking processes in an abstract way. This in itself is a valid purpose.

3.9 A MODERN LOGICAL THEORY ON THE CONDITIONAL STATEMENT

Currently, as far as I know, there is only one other logically-oriented approach active in the psychological field of reasoning. In this approach, Stenning and van Lambalgen (2000, 2008) discuss merely some of the deficient and misleading results that are available so far in the field. The authors handle these results as reliable sources of data and focus primarily on defining the components that explain the large variation in individual responses on the various experimental tasks. According to them, participants in these tasks, for example, in the selection task, must first define the parameters, and the differently chosen parameters produce the variety of answers, many of which, as they say, are correct within the given parameters.

The authors themselves note (2008, p. 111) that the parameters they discuss are difficult to demonstrate experimentally, and they assume that further parameters could be discovered. In this respect, this book also defines such parameters, with markedly significant results, such as, for example, the basic equivalent interpretation of the conditional statement, the avoidance of the selection of all cards and the effect of the alternative antecedents. Of course, the whole literature investigating the relationship between logic and everyday reasoning can be interpreted as the search for and testing of such parameters—components that influence how people resolve tasks.

According to this book, however, the many different answers that appear, for example, in the abstract selection tasks are merely artefacts resulting from the avoidance of the equivalent responses. The same many varied answers that altogether make the preference of P and Q cards also appear in the two evidently biconditional thematic selection tasks discussed in Section 3.1. It is, however, obvious that the equivalent response is the only correct solution in these tasks. So, in the abstract selection task, the search for the parameters that follows the rejection of the correct equivalent response does not necessarily reveal much about the basic inferential processes. Still, it can provide important information on how people try to resolve a situation that was made logically ambiguous.

It is true that in the verbal reports presented by Stenning and van Lambalgen (2008), participants do not speak about avoiding the equivalent response in the abstract selection task. However, if logicians have been unsure about the interpretation of the conditional statement for 2,400 years, lay participants cannot be expected to formulate a clear picture about it in the five to ten minutes that they are given to resolve the tasks. They particularly cannot be expected to be so sure of their interpretation that, on the basis of this, they question the hidden instruction in the selection task, going against the equivalent responses. As a matter of fact, even the good performance on the thematic, easy-to-resolve drinking-age selection task discussed in Section 3.2 drops back by half (from 70% to 35%) by presenting only two P and two not-Q cards to the subjects, hence requiring the turning over of each of them (Veszelka, 1999). This is a statistically significant difference (Pearson Chi-Square $(1, 40) = 4.912$, $p < .027$, Cramer's $V = .350$).

Stenning and van Lambalgen (2008) also address the performance on the conditional statements in Byrne's (1989) so-called suppression tasks. These tasks were already mentioned in Section 2.2. These are the experiments that are based on Geis and Zwicky's (1971) observation with regard to the role of the alternative antecedents. As already discussed, these experiments, in fact, tested the ancient scholastic interpretation of the conditional statement. In doing so, Byrne showed that if we connect a second antecedent to the initial antecedent with an 'or' connective, yet we still express the results only in terms of P and Q, this 'suppresses' the affirmation of the consequent (AC) and the denial of the antecedent (DA) inferences and preserves the modus ponens (MP) and modus tollens (MT) inferences. In this way, we obtain the traditionally accepted conditional inference pattern. She also showed that if the second antecedent is connected to the initial antecedent with an 'and' connective, then in terms of P and Q, this suppresses the MP and MT inferences and preserves the AC and DA inferences.

To interpret these experiments, Stenning and van Lambalgen (2008) assume that the conditional statement could be denoted in the 'If P and nothing abnormal occurs, then Q' form. The insertion of 'nothing abnormal' is a technique in logical programming and can be seen as a paraphrase of the account presented here, where this 'abnormal' component is the additional or alternative second antecedent or consequent.

The authors also handle this 'nothing abnormal' proposition similarly. Through a slightly complicated manipulation, they, in fact, replace it on the antecedent's side with antecedents connected to the original antecedent with an 'and' or an 'or' connective. So, through a number of manoeuvres, they finally use for these tasks the same interpretation found in the present book.

However, I believe it is unnecessary to label these components as 'abnormal'. Such 'abnormal' or 'additional' components can be added to every possible logical statement, even to a stand-alone P statement. Since they can appear everywhere, it is pointless to denote them. Also, the account presented in this book gives the same basic interpretation of the conditional statement for the various experimental tasks (such as the abstract selection task), for the role of additional or alternative antecedents in Byrne's experiments and for the original abstraction of the conditional statement in the antiquity.

In contrast, Stenning and van Lambalgen's (2008) approach is incompatible with how the conditional statement was actually abstracted in the antiquity, and it provides two basically separate explanations for the selection task and for Byrne's suppression tasks. In addition, as far as I know, they do not even address the other three main experimental tasks discussed in this book. For this reason, their theory does not explain why the search for parameters, which, according to them, evokes the wide variation of responses in the abstract selection task, disappears in the inference production task in general, or in the truth table task with dichotomous negatives.

It will also be seen in Section 4 that whereas the approach advanced in this book can also be directly employed to explain performance on syllogisms, Stenning and van Lambalgen (2008) again use a separate approach to explain these results, even if they attempt to embrace all these separate explanations under the umbrella of modern logic.

4 Syllogisms and Euler circles

Despite the noticeable amount of supportive experimental results discussed in Section 3, there were also some bizarre findings, and for this reason, the reader might find that the data are not thoroughly convincing. There is, however, further empirical support, again from a set of fundamental experimental tasks: the approach advanced in this book can also explain the similarly noticeable, experimentally well-demonstrated 'everyday' departures in the other main branch of ancient logic—syllogisms. Syllogisms are based on four types of statements, and one of them—the universal affirmative statement—is treated as equivalent to the conditional statement. It was already seen in Section 2.1 that the classical interpretation of the conditional statement can be traced back to Aristotle, but he is much more often recognised as the founding father of syllogisms.

It is therefore plausible to observe that the same abstraction error that we observed in the case of the conditional statement is also present in the very same form in the abstraction of the universal affirmative statement. The interpretation of two additional statement types in syllogisms, the particular affirmative and the particular negative statements, also need some adjustments.

When fixing these issues, not only do people's so-called everyday inferences become immediately compatible with the rules of syllogisms, but these inferences can also be successfully, clearly and very simply depicted even with Euler circles.

Euler circles are attractively simple but are usually viewed as a rudimentary and, to an extent, inadequate tool to describe syllogisms, both normatively, in prescribing the correct inferences, and descriptively, in describing people's real inferences. However, after making the necessary adjustments, it will be seen that actually, Euler circles can perform very well for both purposes.

The following sections will therefore address these questions. If the reader wishes to immediately proceed to the discussion of some central philosophical problems with regard to the conditional statement in light of the updated scholastic interpretation, he or she can skip Section 4 and continue with Section 5. The reader can return to this section on syllogisms whenever he or she finds it convenient.

4.1   INTRODUCTION TO SYLLOGISMS

Learning the rules of categorical syllogisms (simply 'syllogisms' in the following) is a rather difficult task. In the Middle Ages, learning correct syllogisms was also a mnemonic, a tool for improving memory, similar in this respect to the use of the Latin language.

In syllogisms, there are four types of statements that connect two terms to each other (to create an example sentence which is different than what we have discussed in Section 2, let's say 'dog' and 'happy'). The four possible statements are the universal affirmative statement (e.g. 'All dogs are happy' – All A are B), the universal negative statement (e.g. 'No dogs are happy' – No A are B), the particular affirmative statement (e.g. 'Some dogs are happy' – Some A are B) and the particular negative statement (e.g. 'Some dogs are not happy' – Some A are not B).

Classical syllogisms consist of two premises (that is, of two such statements) and a conclusion based upon them. In addition, the terms can be expressed in the following four orders, the so-called figures, where A and C denote the so-called end terms, and B is the middle term that is present in both statements and connects A and C to each other:

Figure 1	Figure 2	Figure 3	Figure 4
B—A	A—B	B—A	A—B
C—B	C—B	B—C	B—C

Since both premises can be one of the four possible statements, and the figures also have four variants, this makes 4 x 4 x 4, or 64, possible variants in total. The conclusion, which is traditionally in the C–A form, can also be one of the four possible statements, and hence, the number of possible syllogisms increases to 256. Out of this great number of syllogisms, however, Aristotle and scholastic logicians deemed only 24 to be valid (19 and 5 so-called weakened forms), and according to a narrower approach, the number of correct syllogisms is a mere 15 (Copi & Cohen, 1998).

Euler (1768-1772/1842) first began to employ Euler circles, which, according to many authors, such as Blanché (1970, p. 235), can be traced back to Leibniz, to explain syllogisms. He denoted the four possible statements, as shown in Figure 2.

There are two main problems with these traditional Euler circles. One is that from the point of view of logic, except for the universal negative

Universal affirmative statement	Particular affirmative statement	Particular negative statement	Universal negative statement

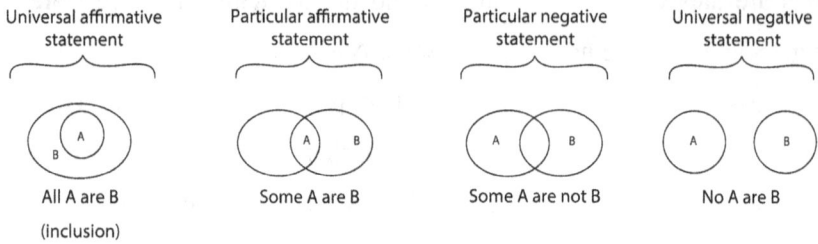

All A are B	Some A are B	Some A are not B	No A are B
(inclusion)			

Figure 2. The traditional denotation of the statement types in syllogisms with Euler circles (based on Shin & Lemon, 2008)

statement, the statements have to be depicted with Euler circles in more than one way to fully cover what a given statement, according to traditional logic, means.

The biggest problem is caused by the particular affirmative statement that, according to the established doctrine, must be expressed with a set of four differently depicted relationships. For example, in the case of 'Some dogs are happy' (Some A are B), it is actually possible that all dogs (A) are included in the set 'happy' (B) as a subset, and it is also possible that the sets 'dogs' (A) and 'happy' (B) fully cover each other, that the 'happy' set (B) is included in the 'dog' set (A) as a subset and that they are intersected (see e.g. Woodworth & Schlosberg, 1954; Stenning & van Lambalgen, 2008). These different relations together represent what the word 'some' means in logic, because in logic, 'some' means 'at least one and possibly all'.

Similarly, in the case of the universal statement, it is assumed that 'All dogs are happy' (All A are B) can refer both to a relationship in which the 'dogs' (A) are included in the set 'happy' (B) as a subset and to a relationship in which they fully cover each other. For such reasons, the

Some A are B

All B are C

syllogism can be, for example, depicted with Euler circles in as many as 16 different ways (Johnson-Laird & Bara, 1984) to determine whether stand-ard logic prescribes a valid conclusion for these premises. This is called combinatorial explosion. Even 16 different representations are extremely difficult to handle, and if we add yet an additional statement, the number of representations quickly becomes impossible to handle.

The notation of the particular statements with Euler circles is also problematic for an additional reason. Euler circles suggest relations that are not attributed to these statements in standard logic. As evident in Figure 2, the 'Some A are B' statement, if depicted with Euler circles, also allows us to read out from this notation that 'Some A are not B', 'Some not A are B' and 'Some not A are not B'. However, according to traditional logic, only 'Some A are B' and 'Some B are A' are equivalents. For such reasons, logicians usually prefer Venn diagrams when they display syllogisms in a figural way.

However, syllogisms do not merely pose problems when someone wants to denote them with Euler circles. A further phenomenon is that in the same way as in the case of the conditional statement, in everyday life, the inferences of people untrained in logic do not correspond to the dictates of logic. In Johnson-Laird and Bara's (1984) Experiments 1 and 3, which focused on 64 syllogisms, used relatively content- and context-independent occupations for the end terms (terms A, C), an interest/preoccupation as the middle term (B), and allowed both A–C and C–A conclusions, the match among the 27 syllogisms deemed valid by the authors and people's most frequent inferences was only 55%.

With respect to the 15 syllogisms still maintained as correct today (Copi & Cohen, 1998), the rate of correct inferences among the most frequent responses is exactly the same, only 55%. Various psychological theories have been introduced to explain this discrepancy, such as the mental models theory (see Johnson-Laird & Bara, 1984; Johnson-Laird, 2006), mental logic (see Rips, 1994), the probability heuristics model (see Chater & Oaksford, 1999; Oaksford & Chater, 2009) or the modern, logical approach of Stenning and van Lambalgen (2008), which stresses the importance of the interpretational components.

4.2 THE ABSTRACTION ERROR IN SYLLOGISMS

However, all of the above problems can be fixed by assuming that the logical abstraction of syllogisms includes the same abstraction error that we have already identified with Aristotle in Section 2.1 with respect to the conditional statement.

As mentioned earlier, this is not by coincidence. Not only can the ancient, scholastic abstraction of the conditional statement be traced back to Aristotle, but he was also the founding father of syllogisms. In addition, the universal affirmative statement in syllogisms is deemed equivalent to the conditional statement. Clearly, Aristotle used the same abstraction for both statements, even though for the conditional statement, this was only an implicit abstraction.

Consequently, the 'All dogs are happy' universal affirmative statement can also be expressed in the form of the 'If a being is a dog, then it is happy' (if P then Q) conditional statement. With Euler circles, both of these are traditionally expressed with the inclusion shown in Figure 2, where 'dog' (set A in Figure 2) is the subset of 'happy' (set B in Figure 2).

We can now also see in a figural way what we have already discussed in Section 2. This inclusion can lead one to deduce the inferences traditionally viewed as correct: because the smaller 'dog' (A) set is included in a larger 'happy' (B) set, from being a 'dog', it necessarily follows that it is 'happy' (modus ponens, MP), and from 'not being happy', it necessarily follows that it is not a 'dog' (modus tollens, MT).

The allegedly incorrect conditional inferences can also be described. It can be seen that from being contained in the larger set 'happy', it does not necessarily follow being also contained in the smaller set 'dog' (affirmation of the consequent, AC), and from being outside of the smaller set 'dog', it is incorrect to infer being necessarily outside of the larger set 'happy' (denial of the antecedent, DA).

In case of the universal affirmative statement, the same can be expressed by saying that because of the inclusion, the 'All dogs are happy' universal statement cannot be converted into the 'All happy beings are dogs' universal statement, but only to the 'Some happy beings are dogs' particular statement.

Yet just as in case of the equivalent interpretation of the conditional statement, it is also a classical observation in syllogisms that people are prone to directly converse the statements (see Wilkins, 1928; Eidens, 1929; Chapman & Chapman, 1959), and in the case of the 'All A are B', they are prone to deduce that this also means that 'All B are A'. So, in fact, the same fallacy can be observed in the case of both the conditional statement and the universal statement. The direct conversion of the universal affirmative statement, creating the 'identity' relation between the two terms, is the same as the equivalent interpretation of the conditional statement. In both cases, the 'dog' and the 'happy' sets fully cover each other.

However, here again, the question arises of why this identity interpretation is interpreted as a fallacy. Why is the set 'dog' only a subset of 'happy', and why do the two sets not fully cover each other? In other words, why is the two-way inference pattern, which people are otherwise prone to follow, incorrect?

The only existing interpretation (see the very citation from Aristotle in Section 2.1, the similar explanation of Jevons, 1906 or that of Brennan, 1961) is exactly the same as that which we have already seen in the case of the conditional statement. It says that, drawing from our present example, other beings can also be happy.

We have already discussed why this interpretation is fallacious: If we refer to another being during the abstraction, we naturally have to denote it. Otherwise, we will violate the basic principle of logic, which is even more fundamental than the abstraction of the basic logical statements and connectives—the requirement to denote all components taken into account in the abstractions.

However, with their denotation, it can be seen again that we are already not characterising a relation between merely two components, 'dogs' and 'happiness', but rather, the relation among at least three terms, which are 'dogs', some other beings (such as 'cats') and 'happiness'. Consequently, with Euler circles, the relationship is the 'happy' set, including 'dogs', 'cats', etc. as subsets, but traditionally, only the sets 'happy' and 'dogs' are denoted.

For exactly the same reasons that we have already seen for the conditional statement in Section 2.2.2, it can be assumed once again that the basic interpretation of the universal affirmative statement, which indeed includes only two elements, can only be the identity. Let us reiterate these reasons.

One is that in the case of having three components, 'dogs', 'cats' and 'happiness', we still commit the 'fallacy' of the direct conversion of the universal affirmative statement: in the case of 'All dogs and cats are happy' (All A and C are B), from 'being happy' (B), we infer 'All dogs and cats' (All A and C). Only *within* 'All dogs and cats' (All A and C) do we not infer specifically 'dog' (A) because it could be 'cat' (C) as well. In other words, in the case of 'All dogs are happy' (All A are B), the direct conversion, as the traditional explanation goes, is invalid merely because of the undenoted 'cat' (C), but if 'cat' is also denoted, the conversion between 'happy' and 'dog and cat' is again valid. If a new, third animal comes to our mind that also happens to be happy, yet we don't denote it, the direct conversion will again be invalid. Denoting it will make it valid again, and so on. Consequently, the direct conversion is not valid only if we have undenoted components. But if we have undenoted components, we should denote them.

The other main argument presented in Section 2.2.2 to support the equivalent interpretation of the conditional statement is also valid here: Let's suppose that one argues that the traditional interpretation of the 'All dogs are happy' statement simply leaves open whether there are alternative terms, such as 'cats', 'cows', etc. on the left side of the statement that could equally lead to the 'happy' term on the right. In such a case, we should note that it is likewise possible that the 'dogs' term on the left leads to additional/alternative terms on the right, such as 'brave' or 'being in a melancholic mood', and yet, this latter, equally valid possibility is not referenced in the traditional interpretation at all. Of course, 'being in a melancholic mood' is in conflict with 'being happy', but so is 'dog' with, for

example, 'cat'. There is no reason to reference possible undenoted components on the left side while neglecting them completely on the right side. It
is also clear that if we reference these undenoted components on the right
side as well, the abstraction will completely lose its sense. With the traditional practice of referring to possible undenoted terms only on the left, at
least some functioning of logic is preserved.

The solution to all these dilemmas is, of course, once again, to simply
denote every instance that is taken into account, either on the left or on the
right, or not to take an instance into account if it is not denoted.

4.3   FIXING THE ABSTRACTION ERROR IN SYLLOGISMS

We have seen in the previous sections that if we assume that the conditional statement must be basically interpreted as referring to an equivalent
relation, we can quite effectively describe the results of the main experimental tasks used in psychology. In Section 5, we will see that this interpretation also resolves the most significant philosophical problems with
regard to the traditional interpretation of the conditional statement, such as
the Raven paradox, the so-called 'paradox of the conditional statement' or
the counterfactuals.

However, fixing the abstraction error does not merely align logic and
people's inferences in the case of the conditional statement. The same happens in syllogisms as well. Furthermore, after making the correction, even
the simplest form of Euler circles develops into an excellent tool to describe syllogisms.

In order to do this, therefore, we must first of all change the inclusion
to identity for the universal affirmative statement; the universal negative

statement remains the same. In the case of the particular statements, they also remain basically the same. The only modification needed here is that, when one or both terms are negated in a particular statement, we explicitly indicate these negated terms in one or both of the labels of the given diagrams. As it follows from the diagrams, each of the four possible particular statements that can be created this way implies their converse and, to an extent, each of them implies one another.

For example, the 'Some A are not-B' statement also means that 'Some not-B are A', and it also implies that 'Some A are B' or 'Some not-A are B'. For historical reasons, however, only the traditional particular affirmative statement 'Some A are B' and the traditional particular negative statement 'Some A are not-B' will be discussed in this book. Whereas this feature of Euler circles is traditionally seen as a major deficiency, it actually allows us to describe people's syllogistic inferences.

Most logical books simply present the interpretation of the universal affirmative statement as an axiom, and the situation is even worse in the case of the particular statements. Just as the word 'all' is differently interpreted in logic than in everyday language, the traditional logical interpretation of the word 'some' also deviates from how it is actually used in natural language. As mentioned, in traditional logic, 'some' means 'at least one and possibly all'. In natural language, people usually do not think 'some' can also possibly mean 'all'. I personally believe that this modified interpretation of 'some' in logic may also follow from the erroneous abstraction of the universal affirmative statement/conditional statement.

As we have already seen, when abstracting the universal affirmative statement, ancient logicians did not realise that the difference between the identity and the inclusion is caused by a third instance. This third instance is not present in identity but is present in inclusion, yet it was not denoted.

Universal affirmative statement	Particular affirmative statement	Particular negative statement	Universal negative statement
A, B	A B	A Not-B	A B
(circle)	(overlapping circles)	(overlapping circles)	(two separate circles)
All A are B	Some A are B	Some A are not B	No A are B
(identity)			

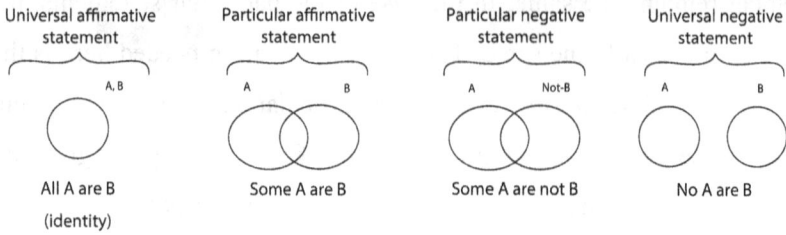

Figure 3. The updated denotation of the statement types in syllogisms with Euler circles

Instead, ancient logicians believed that the universal affirmative statement had two possible interpretations: the 'stronger' identity, when all inferences in both directions are necessary, and the 'weaker' inclusion, where from A, B necessary follows, but from B, A does not necessary follow. It is possible that to play it safe, as we have already seen with Boethius at the end of Section 2.2, ancient logicians prescribed the 'weaker' interpretation of the universal affirmative statement as universally valid. This interpretation guaranteed that people would never endorse inferences that are not always *necessary*. However, these logicians still took into account that the universal affirmative statement can *possibly* also refer to identity. To make this latter possibility compatible with the universally prescribed 'weaker' interpretation of the universal affirmative statement, they said that in some cases, the 'weaker' particular backward inference in the universal affirmative statement, the so-called conversion by limitation, can also refer to the 'stronger' identity. That is, 'some' can also *possibly* mean 'all', or 'some' means 'at least one, and *possibly* all'.

Since in this book, we have identified the real reason for the difference between the identity and the inclusion, and as a consequence, all statements became symmetric and directly convertible, it is unnecessary to differentiate 'weaker' and 'stronger' relations. Correspondingly, it is also unnecessary to assume that 'some' can mean 'at least one and possibly all'.

The summary of these modifications can be seen in Figure 3. These modifications are not merely compatible with people's generally observed tendency in everyday life to directly converse the 'all' quantifier and not to interpret the 'some' quantifier to mean 'possibly all'. A further benefit of this updated approach is that these modifications actually create a very simple overall figural notation for all four statements and remove all the ambiguities of the traditional Euler circles. For example, the particular affirmative statement no longer requires four different diagrams to represent its logical meaning. According to the approach propagated here, one diagram is entirely enough to describe the relation evoked by this statement.

4.4 PEOPLE'S ACTUAL SYLLOGISTIC INFERENCES

Let us now investigate to what extent this updated interpretation can explain people's inferences on syllogisms. With respect to the 64 syllogisms investigated by Johnson-Laird and Bara (1984) in their Experiments 1 and 3, the updated Euler circles shown in Figure 3 give a clean-cut solution in 28 of the cases. Although in the authors' first experiment, the most frequent answers are identical to these 28 solutions in only 16 cases, in their third experiment, the rate is 26 out of 28. Among the total of 14 cases deviating from the rules advocated here, the second-most frequent answers are already all in line with them.

In addition, we can take into account that according to the approach propagated here, both the 'some' and the 'all' quantifiers are bi-directional.

Hence, for instance, the 'Some A are C', 'Some A are not-C' and 'Some C are A' statements on the one hand, and the 'All A are C' and 'All C are A' statements on the other hand, are equivalent, and so we can merge these response options into single responses. When we do so, we naturally get an even better fit. By merging these responses in the first experiment of Johnson-Laird and Bara, only five out of the 28 cases deviate (with an additional three being equal), and only one out of the 28 cases does so in their third experiment. Statistically, the difference would be even less apparent because the differences are often very minimal and would not create statistical significance. But for simplicity, let us use the worst figures with regard to the point of view of the approach advanced in this book and avoid merging any responses.

In the remaining 36 cases, the syllogisms can be depicted with the updated Euler circles in more than one way. In this case, however, we can observe the very simple additional rule that:

> In case of relations that can be depicted in more than one way, we make
> no inference.

This corresponds to the 'no valid conclusion' response option in the experiments of Johnson-Laird and Bara (1984), and even Euler (1768-1772/1842) explained in this way those inferences from which we don't draw conclusions. By adding this rule, people's syllogistic inferences can be described in the same proportion, in 49 out of 64 cases, or 77%, both in Johnson-Laird and Bara's (1984) first and third experiments (see the correspondence between the most frequent answers in these two experiments and the updated Euler circles in Table 10).

In the study of Dickstein (1978), the other experimental database available for all 64 syllogisms that can occur when we don't take into

Table 10. The correspondence between the data of Johnson-Laird and Bara's (1984) Experiments 1 and 3 and the updated rules of syllogisms advanced in this book[*]

Mood[†]	Figure 1	Figure 2	Figure 3	Figure 4
A-A	s ✓✓	s Ø ✓	s Ø ✓	s ✓✓
A-I	s ✓✓	s Ø ✓	s ✓✓	s ✓✓
A-E	s ✓✓	s ✓✓	s ✓✓	s ✓✓
A-O	s Ø ✓	s Ø Ø	s Ø ✓	s ✓✓
I-A	s ✓✓	s ✓✓	s Ø ✓	s ✓✓
I-I	m ✓Ø	m ✓✓	m ✓✓	m Ø Ø
I-E	m ✓Ø	m ✓✓	m ✓✓	m ✓Ø
I-O	m ✓✓	m ✓✓	m ✓✓	m ✓Ø
E-A	s ✓✓	s ✓✓	s Ø Ø	s ✓✓
E-I	m ✓Ø	m ✓Ø	m ✓✓	m Ø Ø
E-E	m ✓✓	m ✓✓	m ✓✓	m Ø Ø
E-O	m ✓✓	m ✓✓	m ✓✓	m ✓✓
O-A	s Ø ✓	s Ø ✓	s Ø ✓	s Ø ✓
O-I	m ✓Ø	m ✓✓	m ✓✓	m ✓Ø
O-E	m ✓✓	m ✓✓	m ✓✓	m ✓Ø
O-O	m ✓✓	m ✓✓	m ✓✓	m ✓Ø

[*]Type of conclusion (simple/multiple), adherence (✓) or deviation (Ø) of the updated interpretation with regard to the most frequent answers in Johnson-Laird and Bara's Experiment 1 and Experiment 3
[†]This column shows the type of the two statements constituting the premises of the syllogisms. A: Universal affirmative statement; I: Particular affirmative statement; E: Universal negative statement; O: Particular negative statement.

account the possible variations in the conclusions, the approach advanced here describes his results in 87.5% of cases both in his Sample 1 and Sample 2. In the case of three premises, with a limited set of syllogisms, the approach presented here is able to describe the results in 81% of cases (Copeland, 2006, Experiment 1) and in 67% of cases (Copeland, 2006, Experiment 2).

For the approximately 20% of responses in general deviating from what is assumed in this book as logically valid, in only three out of 15 cases in Experiment 1 of Johnson-Laird and Bara (1984) but in 13 out of 15 cases in their Experiment 3, the syllogisms did allow several alternatives, and participants favoured one of these alternatives instead of saying 'no valid conclusion'. The same type of erroneous answer appeared in Dickstein's (1978) experiment in 8 out of 8 cases in both his Sample 1 and Sample 2, as well as in 6 out of 6 cases in Copeland's (2006) Experiment 1 and in 10 out of 12 cases overall in his Experiment 2. It can therefore be seen that most of the errors were caused by these erroneous reductions.

This may have something to do with a distorting effect of the experimental material. I believe participants simply may not realise that the given syllogisms have several possible conclusions, or else they believe that providing one possible solution already satisfies the task requirement. It is important to note that, unlike us, participants in these experiments were not equipped with the updated Euler circles offering a quick overview of the given relations. Also, in Johnson-Laird and Bara's (1984) Experiment 1, the data of which deviates the most from the approach propagated here, the results were obtained by allowing the participants only 10 seconds per syllogism. In Experiment 3 of the authors, participants had unlimited time but certainly less than, say, 10 years. In contrast, logicians have spent about 2,400 years on syllogisms and, in one way or another, their views regarding correct inferences can still be questioned.

All things considered, while the psychological experiments are influenced by a considerable number of underlying factors, the at least 77% predictive power nevertheless qualifies as a strong result.

With respect to the 15 officially accepted syllogisms today (see Copi & Cohen, 1998), 11 are still valid in this new interpretation. The four problematic syllogisms are the FERIO (EIO-1), FESTINO (EIO-2), FERISON (EIO-3) and FRESISON (EIO-4) syllogisms. After the names of the syllogisms, the type of statement (E – universal negative, I – particular affirmative, O – particular negative) and the number of the given syllogistic figure can be seen. Using the updated interpretation, the denotation of these four problematic syllogisms with Euler circles is exactly the same, so the problem is also the same in all four cases. In this new interpretation, the relationship between these three sets can be depicted in three different ways, as

Conclusion 1   Conclusion 2   Conclusion 3

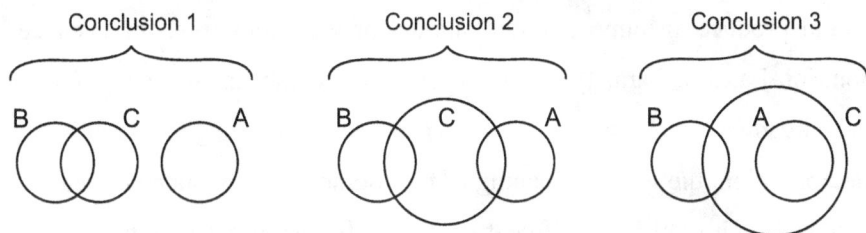

Figure 4. The three possible ways to draw the three sets in the EIO syllogisms

shown in Figure 4.

It might seem that, despite having three possible alternatives, with a little work, the 'Some C are not A' conclusion, which is prescribed by traditional logic as valid, can still be distilled out of the three possible relations. It can be said to be compatible with all the three possible relations. This is, however, not so, because the relations between sets C and A in Conclusions 1 and 3 are incompatible with the new interpretation of 'some'.

In fact, people's inferences show something similar: in the two experiments by Johnson-Laird and Bara (1984), the most frequent answer to these four syllogisms was, in four cases, 'no valid conclusion'; in three cases, participants narrowed the possible relations to the 'No A are C' relation; and in one case, the 'Some C are not A' answer appeared, the answer that is deemed correct in the canon of classical logic.

4.5   THE COUNTERARGUMENT AGAINST EULER CIRCLES IN PSYCHOLOGY

In the literature of cognitive psychology, Euler circles are basically rejected as a tool for describing syllogisms because it is assumed that they would produce an unprocessable amount of variations (see, for instance, Johnson-Laird & Bara, 1984; but cf. Stenning & van Lambalgen, 2008). It has already been discussed in Section 4.1 that, according to the classical interpretation, the logical meaning of the 'Some A are B' statement can be depicted with only four different diagrams. It was also mentioned that in accordance with this, with traditional Euler circles, the following syllogism has to be depicted in 16 different ways:

Some A are B

All B are C

With the interpretation proposed here, however, every statement, even the particular statements, can be depicted in only one way. As a result, even syllogisms with multiple meanings have much fewer and much more transparent variations. According to the new interpretation, the relation above can actually be described in only one way: the sets A and B cover each other partially, and the sets B and C cover each other completely. It follows that set A is partially covered by set C.

Almost everyone infers in this way (see Johnson-Laird & Bara, 1984, Table 9), and in this case, it also coincides with the prescriptions of classical logic. It can also be observed that, contrary to Johnson-Laird and Bara's assumption, processing this syllogism does not require any special modelling/computing capacity from the participants; it is a simple, one-way solution.

4.6   OTHER EVERYDAY SYLLOGISTIC DEVIATIONS AND
THEIR EXPLANATIONS

Whereas we have now a working abstract model for people's everyday syllogistic inferences, it is worth briefly discussing the most popular factors that researchers in psychology have assumed to cause deviations from traditional logic. The most famous of these is the atmosphere effect (see Woodworth & Sells, 1935), the essence of which, according to the description by Woodworth and Schlosberg (1954), is that people are prone to draw inferences that are in the same form as the type of the given premises. For example, in the case of affirmative premises, the inference is also most likely affirmative, and if the type of two premises is the same, then it is probable that the conclusion will also be of the same type.

However, regarding these kinds of observations, Chapman and Chapman (1959) suggested that these could be explained by a simple direct conversion of the statements. The position presented in this book also assumes this. The updated diagrams shown in Figure 3 can all be directly converted, such that all of the statement types are viewed in this approach to be simple two-way relations. Johnson-Laird and Bara (1984) argue against this by saying that if the premises are taken as two-way relations, participants' clear preference for the order of words in the conclusion (such as picking A–C conclusions in the syllogistic Figure 4 and picking C–A conclusions in the syllogistic Figure 1, for instance) cannot be explained. However, premises behave the same way as any other sentence in any language: the order of words has subtle interpretational effects, such as on emphasis, that then also appear in the conclusion.

Others underline the effect of content on syllogisms. Woodworth and Schlosberg (1954) have illustrated this problem with the following syllogism (AAA, Figure 2):

All A are B

All C are B

All A are C

According to traditional logic, this relation does not produce a valid syllogism (see, for instance, Jevons, 1906; Copi & Cohen, 1998). Based on the approach propagated here, however, it is valid, and experimental participants, if drawing a conclusion from these premises, do indeed infer this way (see Johnson-Laird & Bara, 1984, Table 11).

As Woodworth and Schlosberg (1954) argue, replacing A with 'Eskimo', C with 'African' and B with 'having dark hair', it can be seen that the inference 'All Eskimos are Africans' is erroneous. However, if on the other hand, one replaces 'Eskimo' with 'Hottentot', the 'All Hottentots are Africans' conclusion seems correct. The authors interpret this effect as a deceptive phenomenon because, on the basis of the dictates of classical logic, they assume that the inferences are incorrect in both cases.

In effect, however, the two inferences are both valid. The difference only results from a piece of undenoted everyday knowledge, which is nonetheless taken into account when evaluating the characterisations. On one hand, we know that Eskimos do not live in Africa, and the Eskimos (not living in Africa) and the Africans (living in Africa) are thus two opposite concepts. On the other hand, we also take into account, but do not denote, that Hottentots were living in Africa (near the Cape of Good Hope), and so the (African) Hottentots and the Africans are reconcilable concepts. Since, in the case of 'Hottentots', other ethnical groups immediately come to our mind that are likewise living in Africa, the representation of Hottentots does not take place as an identity, but as an inclusion.

A similar example is discussed by Copi and Cohen (1998, p. 262) when reflecting on the rules of categorical syllogisms. In their view, the syllogism

All liberals are proponents of national health insurance

Some members of the administration are proponents of national health insurance

----

Therefore, some members of the administration are liberals

(AII, Figure 2) is invalid. When drawing conclusions in the experiments of Johnson-Laird and Bara (1984), participants mainly accepted this conclusion as valid, and it is also correct on the basis of the approach propagated here (the reader can easily check this by drawing the updated Euler circles for this syllogism).

As the authors wrote, the best way to prove the incorrect nature of this syllogism is to create a logical analogy on the same scheme, which can more easily demonstrate that the conclusion is erroneous. The example they proposed was as follows:

All rabbits are very fast runners

Some horses are very fast runners

Therefore, some horses are rabbits

This syllogism indeed seems more steadily incorrect, but it is not analo-gous to the previous example. In the first example, we know that 'members of the administration' and 'liberals' are not mutually exclusive concepts. Taking into account only these two components alone, these elements could be related to each other in a variety of ways. They can be, for exam-ple, in an identity relation. Alternatively, if other differently politically-oriented members of the administration come to mind, these could be a part of an inclusive relation where administration includes liberals as a subset, or these could be included in a particular relationship if we assume that there are liberals within and outside of the administration and that there are members with varying political orientations within the admin-istration.

In contrast to this, 'rabbit' and 'horse' are mutually exclusive concepts. Thus, in the second case, we clearly have a 'No horses are rabbits' state-ment as well, which is a logically identifiable relationship that, if taken into account, must also be denoted. It is also taken into account because, on the basis of this relation, we find the conclusion to be counterintuitive.

In Figure 5, the two paths of inference can be perfectly followed with the updated Euler circles, and it can be seen that the final outcomes of the two syllogisms are two different relations. In the first case, the form of the universal affirmative statement of the first premise remains the same

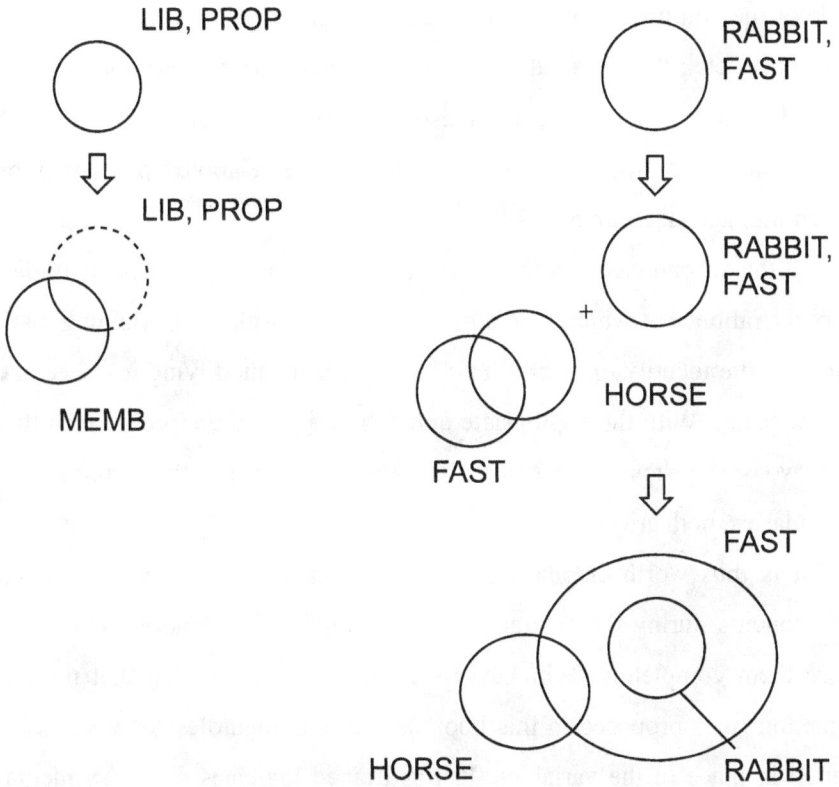

Figure 5. The representation of the logically correct paths of inference and the logically different end forms of two syllogisms deemed both incorrect and logically identical by Copi and Cohen (1998)

throughout the syllogism. The only question may be whether the fully overlapping sets of liberals (LIB) and proponents (PROP) are subsets of the administration (MEMB) or whether these sets are in a particular relationship with each other. As discussed in Section 4.3, however, the particular relationship also implies its converse, which means that there are proponents (PROP) of national health insurance both inside and outside of the administration, and we know only of liberals as proponents. This can be modified only by the additional information that there are no liberals outside of the administration, or there are other proponents of national health insurance, etc.; these are all additional, logically identifiable relationships that, if taken into account, should also be denoted. However, since no such additional information has been denoted, these relationships cannot be taken into account, either.

In the second case, on the other hand, the 'horse', which is contradictory to 'rabbit' but which is in a particular relationship with 'running fast', changes the identity of 'rabbit' and 'running fast', modifying it to become an inclusion. With the appropriate denotation, it can therefore be seen that the two syllogisms are not completely equivalent, and that within their boundaries, both are correct.

It is thus worth emphasising that if we take into account additional components during the abstractions, we should either denote them or ignore them completely. Whichever we chose, it can be seen that the abstraction rules proposed in this book are correct, regardless of what is inserted in place of the variables. Just as trained logicians do, experimental participants most probably also take into account various additional components that come to their minds. This can contribute to the noticeable variations among their responses to the syllogisms, among which this book addressed only the most frequent answers.

4.7   THE MAIN ALTERNATIVE THEORIES ON PEOPLE'S SYLLOGISTIC PERFORMANCE

In the following sections, we will shortly discuss today's predominant theories in the psychological field of reasoning on people's everyday syllogistic inferences to show that the approach presented here is a viable alternative not only experimentally, but also theoretically.

4.7.1   Mental models theory

Although the proponents of mental models theory, as illustrated in Section 4.5, markedly differentiate their approach from the notation with Euler circles, the theory is still only one variant of this notation. The skeleton of mental models theory is a special notation, with which the statements and their interpretations are depicted. In the 1984 version of the theory, the universal affirmative statement was depicted in the following way:

a = b

a = b

0b

These notations are known as mental models. They are read by rows, and each row denotes a co-occurrence. The figure above means that next to every affirmed 'a', there is an affirmed 'b', and the third line, '0b', shows that it is also possible that a 'b' is present without an 'a'. The sign '0' means 'possible'.

Altogether, this figure reproduces the traditional logical interpretation of the universal affirmative statement/conditional statement: the universal affirmative statement can be an identity (if there is no line in which a 'b' value can be displayed without an 'a' value) or inclusion (if a 'b' value can be present in a line without an 'a' value). The relationship between this 1984 variant of mental models theory and the traditional Euler circles can be seen in Figure 6. This figure also displays Leibniz's linear notation, in

Statements	Mental models	Mental models in Euler circles	Euler circles	Leibniz's lines
All A are B	a = b a = b 0b			
Some A are B	a = b 0a 0b			
No A are B	a a b b			
Some A are not B	a a 0a b b			

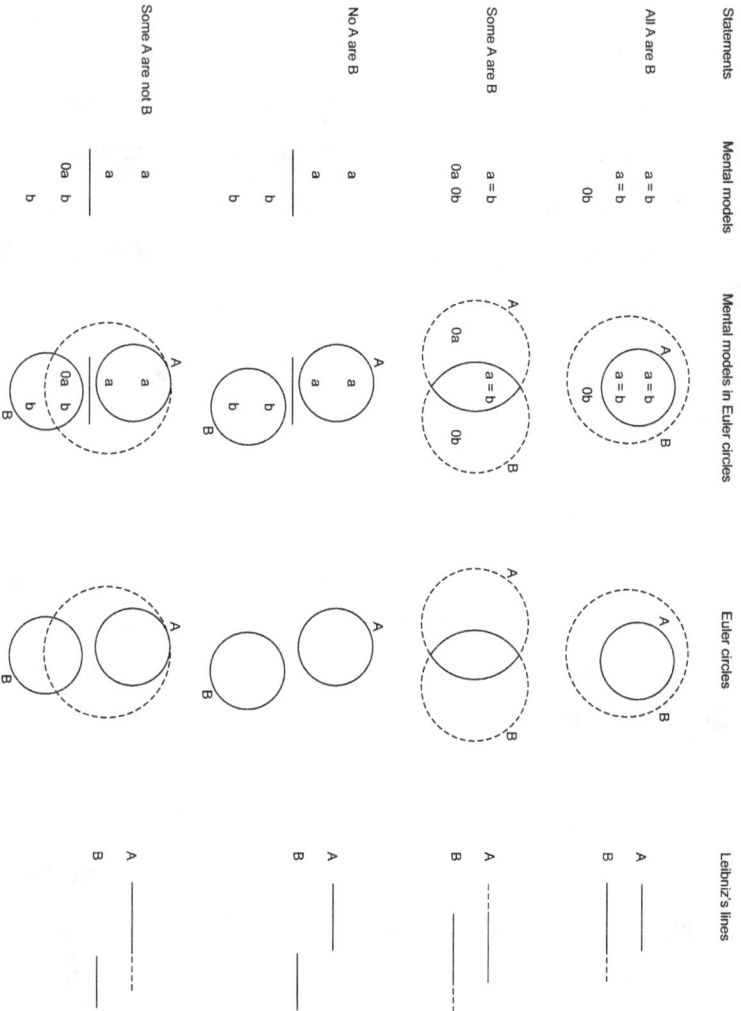

Figure 6. The correspondence between Leibniz's linear and circular notations and the mental models

addition to the circular notation. As mentioned in Section 4.1, the circular notation can also be traced back to Leibniz (see Blanché, 1970, p. 235), but it was lately rediscovered by Euler and became known as Euler circles.

It can be seen that the optional '0' sign in the mental models theory can also be displayed in Leibniz's circular and linear notations with dashed circular arcs or lines. By doing so, the different alternatives of the various statements in syllogisms can be displayed in common figures, just as in the mental models theory. When such dashed lines are used, as was already done previously by many researchers, the difference between Euler's circles and mental models is merely the following: In Euler's circles, we draw circular arcs, and so it is not necessary to display the content of the sets, whereas in mental models, we display the content of the sets, so there is no need to display the circular arcs.

In the same way, if we rotate Leibniz's linear notations by 90 degrees, and we put lines of letters instead of the solid lines and lines of the same letters marked with a '0' sign instead of the dashed lines, we again get the mental models.

This correspondence is not affected by the newer, 1991 version of mental models theory, either (see Johnson-Laird & Byrne, 1991), apart from a small change in the notation, which consists of not denoting with '0' those instances that can appear without other instances, but of using square brackets to denote those instances that cannot. In addition, the negated instances also get denoted. For these reasons, Johnson-Laird and Byrne (1991) had to denote the universal affirmative statement/conditional statement and the equivalence in separate models, which looked like the following:

Conditional		Biconditional	
[p]	[q]	[p]	[q]
[¬p]	[q]	[¬p]	[¬q]
[¬p]	[¬q]		

The reason of explicitly denoting the negated instances was probably that without them, the first line of the universal affirmative state-ment/conditional statement (in the 1984 version, the 'a = b' line) is remi-niscent of the P and Q answers in the abstract selection tasks. This first line in the 1991 version of the theory was presented separately, as follows:

Conditional		Biconditional	
[p]	q	[p]	[q]
...		...	

In this version, this line is called the initial mental model, and the tree dots indicate that further rows containing negated instances may appear. This became, therefore, the explanation of the abstract selection tasks in this theory.

The appearance of the full models displaying the negated instances is explained by the proponents of the theory by the 'fleshing out' mechanism. Sometimes, as in the abstract selection task, no fleshing out occurs, and so people only infer on the basis of the first line. Other times, fleshing out occurs, and people infer according to the full logical patterns.

A noticeable problem is that although this fleshing out mechanism is a fundamental explanatory component of the theory, the exact reason for precisely when and how this fleshing out occurs is still not clarified, even though this problem was raised again and again by other researchers (see, for example, Andrews, 1993; Evans & Over, 1996, 2004; Markovits et al., 1998; Stenning & van Lambalgen, 2008). This may not be a surprise if the explanation of the abstract selection task in the theory is actually merely an analogy that consequently cannot be explained much further.

The proponents of the theory claim that when the negative instances are not explicitly displayed in the models, they are not referenced in the models at all. This, however, also gives some food for thought, because Euler circles also do not explicitly denote the negative instances, yet it is still obvious where these negated instances are. Similarly, in the 1984 version of the mental models theory, where the negated instances were not yet explicitly denoted, the proponents of the theory still assumed that people would know where these instances are.

In Section 3, it was also seen that the P and Q preference in the abstract selection task is probably merely an experimental artefact, and so it does not imply any initial model being present in our thinking processes.

Turning now back to syllogisms, it seems obvious that by merely leaving out the circular arcs, the notation does not become a fundamentally different, semantic notation instead of a logical notation, as the proponents of the theory regularly advocated (see, for example, Byrne, 1989; Johnson-Laird & Byrne, 1991).

In syllogisms, the only benefit of mental models over the notation with circular arcs is that due to their linear lines, they display the linear sequencing of language. In consequence, mental models are able to capture that the syllogisms in the A-B, C-B form are, for example, first transformed by people into a linear A-B, B-C or C-B, B-A sequence, and then they infer on the basis of this sequence. When using the notation with circular arcs, this sequencing, resulting from the sequential nature of language, has to be separately mentioned, as we also did in Section 4.6. Other components of mental models, such as the sources of errors that relate to more response options being present due to more response alternatives ('searching for counterexamples', in the terminology of the mental models theory) and the increased cognitive load because of these alternatives, can, however, already be depicted with Euler circles as well, displaying these response alternatives with dashed lines.

The proponents of the theory also explain people's deviations from the traditionally prescribed interpretations of logic by the erroneous omission of the '0' sign, or in the 1991 version of the theory, that of the square brackets. However, this can also be depicted in Leibniz's circular/linear notations by omitting the dashed lines or by replacing them with solid lines.

Figure 7 shows an example of how a syllogistic inference takes place with mental models, with Euler circles, with Leibniz's lines and by projecting Euler circles and mental models onto each other. It can be seen that the two mechanisms are exactly the same.

Although by reading the literature, it seems that many researchers believe that the mental models theory explains people's syllogistic inferences and that it handles these inferences better than the traditional Euler circles, the two notation methods actually provide exactly the same predictions. This couldn't be otherwise, since, as we have seen, the two notations are, in fact, the same. Accordingly, Johnson-Laird and Bara (1984) do not evaluate their experimental results on the grounds of what mental models predict compared to Euler circles. Instead, they reject Euler circles interpretively before analysing the experimental data, and then they never return to them.

Similarly, the authors did not actually state that the mental models theory explains people's syllogistic inferences, that is, that it predicts how

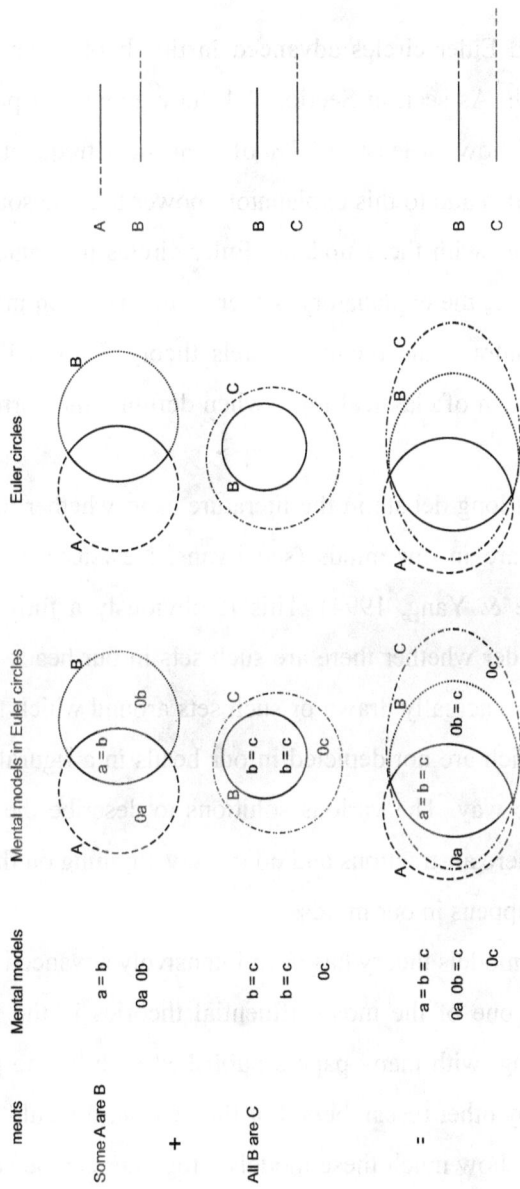

Figure 7. Example of the manipulations with the 1984 version of mental models and with traditional Euler circles in case of a syllogistic inference

people will mainly infer in the cases of the various syllogisms. Instead, they only derive the sources of errors from mental models, as discussed above.

The updated Euler circles advanced in this book seem to be a more precise approach. As seen in Section 4.4, they give exact predictions that people indeed follow, at least in 77% of their most frequent responses. In addition, if we also add to this explanatory power that the sources of errors can be interpreted with these updated Euler circles the same way as with the mental models, the explanatory power of this notation principally rises to 100%. In contrast, the mental models theory follows the traditional, erroneous approach of classical logic when defining the correct syllogistic inferences.

There was a long debate in the literature as to whether logical rules or mental models are in our minds (see Evans, Newstead & Byrne, 1993; O'Brien, Braine & Yang, 1994). This is obviously a futile debate. It is pointless to ponder whether there are such sets in our heads around which the circle arcs are actually drawn or such sets around which they aren't, or perhaps sets which are not depicted in our heads in a figural way but in a linear, linguistic way. The various solutions to describe the inferences in our minds are mere abstractions and do not say anything on this level about what actually happens in our minds.

The mental models theory has been intensively advanced in the past 30 years, and it is one of the most influential theories in the psychological field of reasoning, with many papers published both by the proponents of the theory and by other researchers. For this reason, it would be too large a detour to review how much these models altogether can be separated from Leibniz's circular and linear notations. My impression is that by replacing mental models with Euler circles, not much remains of the theory apart from some interpretative remarks, as it was also exemplified in this section. In the mental models notations of the other main logical components addressed in the psychological literature, such as those of the conditional, the biconditional, the suppression of valid inferences (see Byrne, 1989), the counterfactuals or the illusory inferences (see Johnson-Laird & Savary, 1999), the models and the Euler circles are principally as interchangeable as shown here with regard to syllogisms.

4.7.2   A modern logical theory on syllogisms

Stenning and van Lambalgen (2008) approach the everyday logical inferences in terms of modern logic. Their account of the conditional statement has already been illustrated in Section 3.9. Similarly to the mental models theory, the proponents of this approach also address the syllogisms in terms of Euler circles. However, instead of denoting with dashed lines those parts of the Euler circles where it is optional whether instances are present or not, the authors use solid lines and mark those parts of the Euler circles with an X sign where there must be an instance under every circumstance.

Stenning and Oberlander (1995) wrote that their approach is principally equivalent to what is displayed in the mental models theory. Lately, Stenning and van Lambalgen (2008) have been more critical of the mental models theory, but obviously, it does not make much difference if we denote those parts of the sets with an X where there must be instances under every circumstances, or if we denote those parts with dashed lines or, for example, in the case of the 1984 version of the mental models theory, with a '0' sign, where the presence of instances is optional. Since the authors draw the Euler circles according to the traditional logical interpretation, just as the mental models theory does, their account is also similar to the mental models theory in the respect that it does not explain people's most characteristic answers. Instead, their approach also focuses on explaining the errors compared to this traditional approach.

In contrast to the mental models theory, however, in this approach, the errors are not deduced from Euler circles. Instead, the authors assume that deviations are partly due to Gricean implicatures and partly to the various heuristics assumed by them.

The authors, for example, explain with Gricean conversational implicatures that if someone hears the 'Some A are B' particular affirmative statement, he or she will infer 'Some A are not B' and not 'All A are B'. As the authors argue, because of these conversational implicatures, if someone had in mind a 'stronger' universal affirmative statement, then he or she could use that statement instead of a 'weaker' particular statement. For this reason, when a 'weaker' relationship is stated, people do not infer a 'stronger' relationship.

It can be seen that these Gricean conversational implicatures are also based on the traditional interpretation of syllogisms—according to the approach propagated here, a particular affirmative statement can never refer to a universal affirmative statement. As already discussed in Section 4.3, if we denote all instances taken into account during the characterisations, which is a fundamental principle in logic, we no longer have any reason to differentiate 'weak' and 'strong' relationships in syllogisms. On the contrary, we can provide normative justification for why people do not interpret 'Some A are B' to possibly mean 'All A are B'.

Nonetheless, Stenning and van Lambalgen (2008) only rely on Grice's approach in case of the particular affirmative statement. For the two-directional, identity-type interpretation of the universal affirmative statement that the authors, in line with the contemporary literature, also interpret as fallacious, they argue that this is caused by the fact that people follow 'closed-word reasoning'. According to them, this is a principle which says that in everyday life, we should represent such a model, which is absolutely necessary to understand what has been told (Stenning & van Lambalgen, 2008, p. 313). As the authors explain, in case of the universal affirmative statement, people are prone to take into account only the explicitly mentioned A and B instances, and hence, to infer according to the identity.

The authors do not explain why is it sufficient to take into account only the A and B instances, when according to their approach, this creates erroneous inferences. Yet they almost reached the conclusion advanced throughout this book. In terms of logic, those people are right who only take into account A and B in their inferences when they hear a statement containing only A and B. If they take into account more instances than merely A and B, these instances should either be denoted or else should not be taken into account when drawing the inferences.

However, in the approach of the authors, this remark does not develop into a general, consistent explanation of everyday conditional/syllogistic reasoning. Even in their explanation above, they link this phenomenon to 'closed-word reasoning'.

In addition, whereas in the present book, this basic principle of denoting all instances taken into account during the characterisations was sufficient to explain people's syllogistic inferences in general, the authors assume several additional components to explain the same performance. They do not merely include Gricean implicatures and 'closed-word reasoning', as discussed above, but also various heuristics.

One of the heuristics they posit is that in their inferences, people prefer affirmation over negation. They also assume a practice in which people inferring within a syllogism simply replace the middle term of the syllogism with the end term of the second premise. As these examples have already illustrated, these heuristics are neither logical nor rational. What is more, they can be called heuristics only from the point of view of the authors, since, in fact, the authors are the ones who use these explanations to give heuristic answers (that is, answers that cannot be organically embedded into their approach) to their own theoretical problems.

Because of these heuristics and the other, inconsistent interpretative components illustrated above, it is questionable whether the approach of the authors can indeed be seen as a logical approach. Also, the approach advanced in this present book uses exactly the same interpretation for the conditional statement and for the universal affirmative statement, which is actually in agreement with the general view in logic that handles these statements as equivalent. However, the same cannot be said for Stenning and van Lambalgen's (2008) approach, which, as evident when comparing this section to Section 3.9, uses a different, even though similarly inconsistent, approach to the conditional statement.

4.7.3   Probability heuristics model

In the third alternative approach currently popular in the field, Chater and Oaksford (1999) state that people's syllogistic inferences are not logical, but are still rational. As they argue, these inferences indicate that people choose the most informative components, or at least infer on the basis of them. As already seen in Stenning and van Lambalgen's (2008) approach, the authors also assume heuristics to explain the experimental results. Such a heuristic is, for example, that the quantifier of the conclusion should be the same as the less informative premise (Chater & Oaksford, 1999, p.

197), or that if the less informative premise has an end-term as its subject, it is then used as the subject of the conclusion (p. 198).

The authors deduce these heuristics from the universal affirmative statement > most (a statement type added by the authors) > few (another statement type added by the authors) > particular affirmative statement > universal negative statement > particular negative statement ordering. They argue that the statements in syllogisms are informative in this order.

However, just as in the case of Stenning and van Lambalgen's (2008) approach, these heuristics are again heuristics from the point of view of the authors only. They do not look very rational. Although Chater and Oaksford (1999) attempt to give a rational explanation for the ordering they made on the basis of informativeness, these are merely postulates. For example, they point out that in the world, things are principally not identical to each other; for this reason, the universal negative statement is very frequent and as such, not informative. Consequently, it is placed at the end of the sequence shown above. The authors do not prove that things in the world are less related to each other in a particular affirmative or inclusive relationship. In fact, the way the authors explain syllogisms suggests that they deduced the heuristics they advance from the existing experimental results, and then they used these heuristics exceptionally to explain these experimental results. This raises the risk of circularity. This is particularly so, for in Section 6.2, it will be seen that the explanation that the authors propose for the abstract selection task also risks circularity.

4.7.4   Summary of the main alternative theories

In sum, the three perhaps most dominant theories that currently prevail in the psychological field regarding people's everyday syllogistic reasoning explain the results only partially and inconsistently. The mental models theory (see Johnson-Laird & Bara, 1984; Johnson-Laird & Byrne, 1991) is propagated as a non-logical, semantic theory, but it is merely an alternative notational variant of Euler circles. The basic skeleton of the modern logical approach of Stenning and van Lambalgen (2008) does not seem to rely on modern logic, but rather on various questionable and inconsistent philosophical interpretations and even on heuristics that are neither logical nor rational. Finally, the similar heuristics of the probabilistic-heuristic model of Chater and Oaksford (1999) even raise the risk of circularity.

By contrast, the approach suggested in this book has solid efficiency in describing the results. It is consistent, logical and rational. In addition, it explains the experimental results in such a way that can be immediately linked to the explanation of other experimental results, and as it will be seen in the following, to many current philosophical/theoretical questions relating to the conditional statement/universal affirmative statement.

Finally, the approach advanced in this book is the only approach in the field that takes into account how the conditional statement and the universal affirmative statement were actually abstracted in the antiquity. In the case of the conditional statement, some might disagree that modern mathematical logics are also based on the ancient abstraction, and so the ancient abstraction is, in general, relevant to today's logic, even though there are clear signs of this, as seen in Section 2.2 with regard to propositional logic.

However, when it comes to syllogisms, it is impossible to deny even for them that these statements have been abstracted in the antiquity. It is therefore reasonable to take into account how this abstraction was actually made. Now, if we take this into account, and we see the same abstraction error as in the conditional statement, how can we deny that they are interrelated, and as such, that both of them have to come from the same source? How can we deny this, especially when even modern logic treats the conditional statement and the universal affirmative statement as equivalent? I believe these connections pose serious problems to those logicians who contemplate the traditional abstractions of logic as unquestionable axioms.

4.8   SUMMARY OF SYLLOGISMS AND EULER CIRCLES

As it was seen, after fixing the abstraction error in the universal affirmative statement and adjusting the interpretation of the particular statements, Euler circles evolve into an exceptional tool for describing the everyday performance on syllogisms. With the help of these diagrams, people's syllogistic inferences can easily be traced and can quite effectively be explained and predicted. Every statement used in syllogisms can be exclusively identified with a given relationship between two Euler circles. If there is no better argument in the history of logic as to why the universal affirmative statement is interpreted as an inclusion and why the particular statements are interpreted the way that they are, these inferences are also valid from the point of view of logic. In the case of the universal affirmative statement, the abstraction error is quite obvious, and in the case of the classical interpretation of the particular statements, the traditional approach may also ensue from this erroneous interpretation.

In addition to providing a sophisticated tool to quickly describe and predict everyday syllogisms, the updated Euler circles also allow us to approach some other interesting questions. One of these is whether, on the basis of the updated interpretation, an inclusion can exist at all between only two components. In my view, the existence of such a relation is very limited. Any time we observe an inclusion between only two components, we can begin to look for the third component that transforms the identity into an inclusion. The transformation of identity into inclusion could already be seen in the 'rabbit-horse-running fast' example in Figure 5. Euler circles provide a great visual tool to denote how such new components appear in our minds, and as such, can offer a starting point to visually represent more complex phenomena, such as learning, belief revision or everyday/scientific discoveries. The new notation also allows us to process syllogisms with more than three premises, whereas the traditional notation is, in principle, unable to handle them.

If there is hesitation in calling this approach a logical approach, then the approach can be merely viewed as an abstract set of rules, or even as a heuristic model, that describes everyday human syllogistic inferences in an abstract way. The main point is not about how we label something, but about how it actually works. Traditional logic performs poorly when trying to understand how people actually draw their logical inferences, which is a problem if we want to use it to describe it.

According to the traditional view, the aim of the classical Greco-Roman/scholastic logic was not to describe people's inferences, but rather, to define the correct argumentation in case of disputes. Similarly, in modern philosophical logic, it is maintained that the purpose of logic is to set forth 'ideal' inferences. However, when defining these, logicians undoubtedly wanted to establish *correct* rules. On the other hand, people resolving experimental tasks based on these logical components are obviously giving answers that they deem to be *correct*. Consequently, there are no real differences between defining the correct/ideal argumentation and 'everyday' reasoning.

For example, when Aristotle defined the rules of syllogisms, he probably defined them in a way that he believed was valid. Successive logicians also accepted them as valid because they agreed with them, and then made modifications to them, such as with regard to the existential import (which was not discussed in this book), because they believed they would be correct. There is no eternal truth involved in this, except that we are perhaps heading towards this eternal truth by carefully considering the explanations that were brought forward to underpin the traditional interpretations.

Consequently, if a logician can prove that it makes sense to denote only some of the propositions and not others, then normatively, the account presented in this book can be questioned and maybe even seen as logically not valid. But even then, this approach will be still a possible way to describe people's 'everyday' inferences in an abstract way, which is at least as important as giving an interpretation that can be accepted as normatively valid.

Nowadays, more and more studies demonstrate the interdisciplinary rapprochement between logic and psychology (see Edgington, 2003; Evans & Over, 2004; van Benthem, 2008; Fisher, 2008; Stenning & van Lambalgen, 2008; Oaksford & Chater, 2010; Novaes, 2012). This book argues that ancient logic is also a connection point, particularly as all logical components currently studied in psychology—that is, being recognised by psychologists as relevant to the discipline in the past 100 years—have already been defined in the antiquity and have remained basically the same ever since. As already mentioned in the Introduction and as discussed throughout this book, this is especially worth considering because these abstractions took place in a linguistic, psychological, philosophical context instead of a mathematical one. It would therefore be very natural for philosophers, linguists, psychologists and logicians interested in human sciences to address the roots of their respective sciences and to investigate and, if appropriate, fix these ancient abstractions.

5 Philosophical considerations

In the previous sections, we have reviewed the way the conditional statement and the universal affirmative statement were abstracted in the antiquity, as well as exactly what error was committed in this abstraction. We
also reviewed the main experimental tasks of psychology on the conditional statement and on syllogisms. It can be seen that the basic equivalent
interpretation of the conditional statement/universal affirmative statement
and the denotation of the propositions taken into account during the abstractions allowed us to explain these experimental results within a unified
theoretical framework. Among others, it was experimentally demonstrated
that people basically interpret the conditional statement as an equivalence,
and with an additional, alternative antecedent, this evolves into the
relationship that is traditionally accepted for the conditional statement to be
logically valid. It was also seen that this can be easily connected to the way
people interpret syllogisms. In Section 4.7, we also saw that this approach
can more consistently explain people's everyday syllogistic inferences than
the main alternative theories in the psychological field of reasoning.

But how all of these relate to the most important philosophical questions relating to the everyday, natural language interpretation of the conditional statement will be explored in the next sections. We will address
some further alternative approaches and will investigate the basic equiva-

lent interpretation with regard to questions that, just as has already happened several times in this book, seemingly contradict it, such as the paradox of the conditional statement, the Raven paradox, the counterfactuals or the probabilistic interpretation of the conditional statement.

5.1   NON-MONOTONIC ASPECTS

Many researchers assume that the description of human inferences necessitates the introduction of non-monotonic logics. Accordingly, not only is Stenning and van Lambalgen's (2008) modern logical approach, discussed in Sections 3.9 and 4.7.2, non-monotonic, but as we already discussed in Section 2, the approach propagated here also has similar characteristics. For example, in Section 2.1, we accepted the soundness of the MP inference. Then, in Section 2.2, as a consequence of a second antecedent being connected to the initial antecedent with an 'and' connective, we rejected it. Therefore, we revised our belief, which is a key phenomenon to tackle with non-monotonic logics.

Also, it follows from the account presented here that in 'everyday' life, in fact, no conditional relationship can exist between just two components. If we still observe it, we can start looking for the third component that makes the equivalent relation into a conditional relation. This connects the approach to learning processes and does so in the very roots of logic. It is therefore important to note that these non-monotonic features arise merely by fixing an ancient abstraction error. Obviously, this suggests that if logic had been abstracted correctly in antiquity, it would have been non-monotonic by its very origin. Nonetheless, it is never too late to fix a mistake.

Today's non-monotonic logics—such as default logic (see Reiter, 1980) and defeasible logic (see Nute, 2003)—are introduced on one hand to address such belief changes, and on the other hand, to tackle the various aspects of the frame problem, or in other words, computational tractability. The frame problem is that we can enlist a practically infinite number of propositions that possibly influence a given state of affairs, but in a specific case, most of them can be considered irrelevant or remain true by default. Contrary to today's non-monotonic logics, the approach propagated here has no built-in apparatus to limit the number of propositions. It currently allows an infinite number of propositions to come to mind, such that we are able to enlist a practically infinite number of propositions dependent on having sufficient capacity or time. So, it is assumed here that capacity and time are limited, not the logical or deductive system per se.

The aforementioned non-monotonic logics avoid the denotation of the large number of possibly occurring components by denoting only default or typical consequences. However, it is also an option to denote all propositions if and when they come to mind, provided that the limits of our computing capacity are addressed in a separate, more general model, of which this logical apparatus is only an important part.

5.2   BASIC CONTEXTUAL EFFECTS

Several examples have already been discussed in this book showing the common practice in the literature of leaving the context undenoted. All of this can perhaps be seen as acceptable for mathematical purposes, where context has practically no influence on the inferences.

However, the undenoted context—and the related monotonic interpretation of logical truth and logical necessity—is also a heritage of the classical Greco-Roman logic that, in consequence of the erroneous abstraction of the conditional statement, was rigid and unable to develop, and did not allow for proper description of the effect of context. When fixing this error, the basic effect of the context can immediately be seen, even when the equivalent relationship transforms into a conditional relationship—and this can be quite precisely described.

Several examples of this have been provided in this book, even with two mathematical sentences in Section 2.2.1 and with a mathematical content presented in the 'conditional' and 'equivalent' abstract problems in Experiments 2, 3, 4 and 5. As seen, for example, in Experiments 4 and 5, the conditional statement can even be exactly the same and can still trigger either conditional or equivalent responses, depending merely on the background context; in this specific case, it is on whether the number '3' or '6' was displayed to the participants. It was also seen that these underlying relationships can be precisely described; they do not require the introduction of a specific apparatus, just because the conditional statement in one of the cases evoked an equivalent, and in the other case, a conditional relationship, and with the addition of further contextual components, could behave again in quite a different way.

I believe that more complex contexts and even the concepts themselves behave in accordance with the same principle. Naturally, in more complex case, we cannot predict the exact context or conceptual network in someone's mind, but without precise information, we cannot predict which numbers are being added in someone's mind, either. We can make only vague or probabilistic predictions, just as happens in the case of the vague

or probabilistic approaches of the conditional statement. However, addition
and subtraction written down on paper are still very useful tools.[3]

---

[3] In addition to the dilemma of the conditional statement, the second most
intriguing question regarding the everyday interpretation of the basic logical
connectives is what decides when an 'or' connective is interpreted as an exclusive
'or' and when it is interpreted as an inclusive 'or'. In an exclusive 'or', the
disjunction is true only if one of the two disjuncts being connected together with
the 'or' connective is true but is not true when both of the disjuncts are true. In
case of an inclusive 'or', the disjunction is true also when both disjuncts are true
(for this reason, it is called 'inclusive' and the other 'exclusive'). This question
also has its own literature. When in the realm of human sciences, we are also
allowed to take into account the effects of concepts when thinking about logic, it is
easy to find a simple solution to this dilemma. The 'or' connective is interpreted as
an exclusive 'or' when the two disjuncts exclude each other (for example, 'dog or
cat') and is interpreted as an inclusive 'or' when the two disjuncts can coexist at
the same time (for example, without any additional context, 'milk or bread'). It is
that simple. On a more technical level, I believe the concepts can be denoted the
same way as any other contexts, and so, in the case of the exclusive disjunction,
the conflicting propositions can be denoted and can then be instantly analysed with
the content-independent, abstract rules of logic. The analysis of concepts is also
required because the background context inherent to them explains why in the 'if P
then Q' statement, the instances P and Q are different even though they are stated
to be equivalent/identical on the level of the 'if-then' connective or the universal
affirmative statement. Mathematical logics also acknowledge that an equivalent
relation can exist between two different terms, but without entering into the
analysis of concepts, it is impossible to explain how two different terms can be
equivalent at the same time.

5.3 THE PARADOX OF THE CONDITIONAL STATEMENT

The interdisciplinary literature is not merely characterised by the erroneous practice of taking into account additional propositions that are at the same time left undenoted. This is coupled with discerning no difference between sentential truth (what is true according to the formulated sentences themselves); the truth in one's mind (what is true according to one's experiences); and the truth in the real world (what is true in reality).

The most marked example of this is when, for example, the 'unicorn exists' statement is given. It is then noted that however puzzling such a case may be, since this statement is false, it follows that whatever statement is added to it as a consequent, the created conditional statement will be true. This is interpreted to follow from the traditional interpretation of the conditional statement in propositional logic (as shown in Table 1). In this case, a negated antecedent always makes the conditional statement true, regardless of the consequent and as Frege (1918-19/1984, pp. 400-401) explained, regardless of how odd it sounds in everyday language.

Although this so-called paradox of the conditional is indeed very odd, the source of the oddity—next to the erroneous abstraction—follows once again from undenoted propositions. If we deliberately forget everything we know about the unicorn and solely consider the assertion just as it figures in the example, without denoting any further propositions, then there are no components with which this assertion can be considered contradictory, and thus, it cannot be true or asserted. Frege's purpose was also to remove such 'adjuncts' from the abstractions. This is an idea worthy of support.

After allowing that the 'unicorn exists' can be affirmed, the basic equivalent interpretation resolves what still remains of the paradox: the negated antecedent does not make the conditional statement generally true.

It makes it true only when the consequent is also negated. When the consequent is affirmed, the negated antecedent makes the conditional false.

The same applies to the other way of expressing the paradox, to the assumption that the affirmed consequent always makes the conditional statement true, regardless of the antecedent. According to the equivalent inference pattern, this is not so, either; in the case of an affirmed consequent, an affirmed antecedent makes the conditional statement true, and a negated antecedent makes it false.

5.4   FURTHER EXAMPLES OF THE UNDENOTED CONTEXT

In a recent paper, Krzyżanowska, Wenmackers and Douven (2013, p. 315) argue that the antecedent and the consequent of the conditional statement—at least, as they say, in many cases —must have an inferential connection with each other. This assumption has a long history (see, for example, Tarski, 1946/1995, pp. 24-26). The authors exemplify this with statements in which one or two of the premises are generally true in everyday life. They use the following statement as an example:

'If badgers are cute, then 2012 was a leap year.'

They assume that in this example, the connection is missing, and this explains why people are reluctant to accept it.

In this book, it is assumed that the 'if-then' statement always creates an equivalent connection between the antecedent and the consequent. For those who want to use logic to formalise psychology or to program it into a machine, it is important to avoid classifications and typologies on the basic connectives unless they are absolutely necessary. In agreement with this, the only reason we find the connection between 'cute badgers' and '2012 as a leap year' as non-existent is that we know from everyday experience that finding animals cute is independent of when leap years occur. However, as soon as we have such a premise in our mind—and we have it in our mind, as we will give a similar explanation if asked why, in fact, there is no inferential link between cute badgers and leap years—we should either denote it or ignore it completely when analysing the conditional statement.

Doing so, then, we can describe the presence or the lack of the 'inferential link' by keeping the basic equivalent interpretation of the conditional statement, without the need to introduce a typology: either we do not take into account the additional premise and don't denote it, thus endorsing the equivalent conditional inferences, or we take into account the undenoted premise but then must denote it, and in terms of P and Q, we no longer endorse the equivalent inferences. The typology advanced by this group of authors (see Douven & Verbrugge, 2010 for further examples) is generally dependent on such undenoted context.

The undenoted context has even been used to argue against the basic equivalent interpretation of the conditional statement. For this purpose, Sanford (1989, p. 236) mentions the 'If someone thinks that his beliefs and desires are controlled by radio waves from the planet Venus, that person has at least heard of Venus' conditional sentence, where the equivalent inferences, such as the affirmation of the consequent inference, appears problematic. Hence, according to the author, it undermines the general equivalent interpretation. However, the reason for this is that once again, we are well aware, but do not denote, that there are other groups of people not identical to those mentioned in the antecedent who have equally 'at least heard' of the planet Venus.

Grice's (1975) maxims also rely on such undenoted context. The 'be co-operative', 'relevant' and 'truthful' or the 'maxim of quantity' are very general expectations during conversations that influence communication without being explicitly stated. I believe these rules are learned during childhood, much the same way as, for example, the rules that regulate how we travel on the streets. Yet in addition to the statements explicitly stated during conversations, these maxims can also be denoted and then can be instantly analysed with the tools of logic. Obviously, denoting them is as valid an option as leaving them undenoted and interpreting them as a pragmatic effect that cannot be handled in terms of logic.

Grice's maxims were also used to explain some of the allegedly fallacious inferences in syllogisms. We have already discussed this in Section 4.7.2. In fact, Grice also has an interpretation of the paradox of the conditional statement. His explanation relies on the general assumption that the 'if P then Q' statement, if traditionally understood, is equivalent to the 'not-P or Q' statement. Then, according to his approach, in case of the 'if the unicorn exists, then Peter will come' conditional statement, the paradox ensues because the speaker in fact says that 'either the unicorn doesn't exist or Peter will come'. However, as it is told, everyone knows that the 'unicorn doesn't exist', which violates the communication maxim of not saying a statement that is weaker than what the speaker actually assumes to hold (see, for instance, Edgington, 2008; Fisher 2008). This can perhaps be seen as an impressive explanation, but it does not take into account that sentential truth and truth in the real world are two separate things. In fact, the explanation does not even tell why we feel the above statement implies that 'Peter will not come'.

It is true that this indeed does not follow from the traditional interpretation. This traditional interpretation sees the 'if P then Q' conditional statement equivalent to the 'not-P or Q' statement so that the 'or' connective is interpreted as an inclusive 'or', which, as we have already discussed in Footnote 3, means that either one or both disjuncts can be true to make the disjunction true, and the disjunction is false only if both disjuncts are false. Since, according to the traditional interpretation, 'the unicorn doesn't exist' is true, it can follow both that 'Peter comes' and that 'Peter doesn't come'. The same applies to the traditional interpretation of the conditional statement, where from the false antecedent, we can infer both the affirmed and the negated consequent (as seen, for instance, in Table 1). Some researchers (such as Edgington, 2003 and Evans & Over, 2004) say that in everyday life, we don't infer from the negated antecedent, but these approaches again do not explain why we feel in this specific case that 'Peter doesn't come'.

This problem, once again, disappears with the basic equivalent interpretation. In this interpretation, from the false antecedent 'the unicorn doesn't exist', it follows that 'Peter will not come'. From the 'unicorn exists', it follows that 'Peter will come', but we know from everyday experience that the 'unicorn doesn't exist'. If we denote this additional proposition, and so we are allowed to take it into account during the characterisation as well, we have no other option than to conclude that 'Peter will not come'. Similarly, the biconditional 'if P then Q' relation is equivalent to the 'not-P or Q' statement only if, contrary to the general assumption, we interpret the 'or' connective as an exclusive 'or'. In the exclusive 'or', the two disjuncts cannot both be true. Consequently, if the 'unicorn doesn't exist' statement is true, we are forced to infer that 'Peter will not come'.

Finally, to mention some additional examples, in sentences such as 'If you are thirsty, there is some soda in the refrigerator', it indeed follows that 'If you are not thirsty, there is no soda in the refrigerator' (DA inference). This can be seen as absurd only because of our everyday experience, which tells us that being thirsty does not influence whether there is soda in the refrigerator or not. However, as soon as we denote this additional information, or any other information that comes to mind, the phenomenon can be instantly analysed in terms of logic.

The same happens in statements such as 'If you remember, we saw that cat yesterday'. Here, from the fact that 'we saw that cat yesterday', it follows that 'you remember' (AC inference). However, from our everyday experience, we know that experiencing an event together is not a guarantee that everyone always remembers it, and particularly not that everyone simply remembers in general. There is only one way to resolve these absurd inferences: if we complete the sentence into its original form: 'If you remember it, you can recall that we saw that cat yesterday'. In doing so, we can already infer according to the equivalent inference pattern as usual.

As a final example of this sort, let us consider the 'if Aristotle wrote any dialogues, they have not survived' (Read, 1995, p. 64) sentence. Without considering the context, this could again be a good counterexample against the views expressed in this book. In this statement, the denial of the antecedent, the assertion that Aristotle did not write dialogues, and hence, they have survived (not-P and not-Q), is a nonsense inference. However, once again, the nonsense nature of this inference ensues from our everyday experience telling us that non-written dialogues cannot survive (not-P and Q). From this contradictory (if not-P then not-Q and Q) situation, either the solution suggested by our experience wins, where we redundantly infer the Q consequent from the not-P antecedent, or, owing to the contradiction, our thought process simply stops at not-P, and seemingly, we don't infer at all.

5.5   HEMPEL'S RAVEN PARADOX

Denoting the context and the basic equivalent interpretation also resolves Hempel's Raven paradox. In this paradox, we analyse the 'All ravens are black' universal affirmative statement, which, as we have already discussed when discussing syllogisms in Section 4, is equivalent to the 'If it is a raven, it is black' (if P then Q) conditional statement. According to traditional logic, this conditional statement means the same as the 'If it is not black, it is not a raven' statement (if not-Q then not-P). This remains true even with the equivalent interpretation of the conditional. As it is commonly explained, the dilemma arises if we take into account, for example, a green parrot (non-black and non-raven). As it is told, a bird with such an appearance confirms the conditional, even though it has nothing to do with black ravens.

However, this is not so, as by taking into account green parrots in addition to black ravens, the former also need to be denoted, since we obviously took them into account during the characterisation. In such a case, since we only have parrots and ravens, and since we only have green and black colours, given that only these are denoted, the basic equivalent interpretation of the conditional statement makes these opposites by elimination. Correspondingly, the green parrot indeed confirms the black raven.

We have already seen the same at a very elementary level in the experiments on people's abstract everyday conditional inferences, when dichotomous negatives were used in an abstract truth table task, simple inference task, and inference production task (see Tables 2 and 3 in Section 3.1). In these tasks, which—in the experiments that I conducted—had the possible values of 'A' and 'K' for the antecedent and the possible values of

'3' and '4' for the consequent, the most characteristic inference of the participants was the equivalent inference pattern.

Still, some people might argue that the real paradoxical nature of the raven paradox arises when we imagine countless other non-black non-ravens, such as, for example, yellow ducks, grey dolphins, etc. The more such components we have, the more it seems paradoxical that the confirmation of one of them confirms that all ravens are black.

However, by denoting these additional components, we can instantly see why. Let's add, for example, the 'yellow duck' to the 'black raven' and the 'green parrot' discussed above. Suppose that we start to test the 'All ravens are black' statement in such a context, and we find a 'green duck'. In addition to the duck, this co-occurrence only affects the parrot that was originally said to be green: either the green colour cannot be exclusively linked to the parrot—as the initial basic equivalent relationship would imply—or if there is an artificial one-by-one correspondence between the animals and the colours, which is not defined in the Raven paradox, then the parrot already cannot be green. The raven, however, can still be both black and yellow (or if there is no one-by-one correspondence between the colours and the animals, even green). This means that when falsifying this 'non-black non-raven' pair, the 'All ravens are black' statement can still be both true and false.

The same way, if we find a co-occurrence that verifies the 'yellow duck', the raven could still be both black and green (or if there is no one-by-one correspondence between the colours and the animals, even yellow), so once again, the initial 'All ravens are black' statement can still be both true and false.

This is why, when we have more than two colours and animals, only checking the ravens (and because of the equivalent interpretation, the black things) reveals something about the truth of the 'All ravens are black' statement. The other pairs are informative only if one of their members is hidden, and then if this hidden member happens to be a raven or a black thing. However, the more animal-colour pairs we have, and the larger these groups are, the lower the chance of finding such hidden instances. This is why it's easy to associate probabilities when studying the Raven paradox, and this is why, for example, Oaksford and Chater (2010) also note with a different example that the non-black non-ravens seem irrelevant when evaluating the truth of the 'all ravens are black' statement.

In Section 3.1, we have already seen the same phenomenon in the abstract truth table and simple inference tasks with implicit negatives. In that section, this phenomenon was labelled an 'enumerative' interpretation, but we have now discussed how this 'enumerative' interpretation emerges from the basic equivalent interpretation due to an undenoted context.

5.6   COUNTERFACTUALS

Many researchers divide the conditional statements into two main categories, indicative conditionals and counterfactual conditionals. In this book, we have so far discussed the indicative conditional statements only. The most popular example sentences of these two different types of conditionals are as follows (see Adams, 1970; Evans & Over, 2004; Edgington, 2007, 2008):

a) If Oswald didn't kill Kennedy, someone else did;

b) If Oswald hadn't killed Kennedy, someone else would have.

The first statement is indicative, the second is counterfactual. It can easily be seen that the counterfactual conditional statement functions differently than the indicative conditional statement. In case of (a), we can easily endorse the equivalent inferences, such as the denial of the antecedent inference (if Oswald did kill Kennedy, someone else did not); in the second case, however, we encounter a problem. If we also simply negate the antecedent and the consequent in this sentence to endorse the denial of the antecedent inference (If Oswald had killed Kennedy, someone else wouldn't have), we get a statement that is exactly the opposite of the initial conditional statement, and not a conditional statement that can be reconciled with it, as in case of the (a) statement.

Since other researchers do not build their arguments around the basic equivalent interpretation, and in their approaches, sentential truth and truth in the real world are not differentiated from each other, they explain the variation differently (see, for example, Read, 1995; Byrne & Tasso, 1999; Evans & Over, 2004; Edgington, 2007). They, for example, say that whereas the (a) statement can be accepted as true, the (b) statement can appear as false. Nonetheless, because of such differences between the indicative and the counterfactual conditional statements, many believe that it is impossible to give a unified account of the everyday interpretation of the conditional statement. Since in this book, it is assumed that the basic interpretation of the conditional statement is always the equivalence, it is worthwhile to briefly discuss the question of counterfactuals.

What we must first of all clarify is that, contrary to what is assumed, the counterfactuals are actually not a subset of the conditional statements. We can formulate counterfactuals even with simple sentences such as 'the sun could have shone', or we can say that:

c) You could have gone with them, or you could have taken a coat.

This is a counterfactual disjunction, and so on. Therefore, a counterfactual can be formulated for all possible statement types, not only for the conditional statement. The role of the counterfactual is the following: we can speak about logical relations in the past as closed connections or as open connections that are subject to investigation. The closed relations are the indicative statements, and the statements that clarify or establish additional connections in the past ('what could have been') are the counterfactuals.

Another property of the counterfactual statements is related to this. If someone formulates such a statement, he or she indicates at the same time that the opposite of that has actually happened. For example, if we say that 'the sun could have shone', it also means that in reality, the sun did not shine. The same applies to the (c) counterfactual disjunction, which says that 'you did not go with them and you did not take a coat'. Similarly, in case of the (b) counterfactual conditional statement, with the antecedent 'if Oswald hadn't killed Kennedy', we also say that 'Oswald had killed Kennedy'. Behind every counterfactual and so also behind every counterfactual conditional, there is such a statement about the past. This is not a surprise, since exactly this statement is that 'fact' against which we formulate the counterfactual. We cannot reconstruct such a background statement for indicative conditionals.

This is an important difference. Researchers are aware of these background statements (see Fillenbaum, 1974; Read, 1995; Byrne & Tasso, 1999) and often even take them explicitly into account, but still, they do not denote them. Frank Jackson's or Davis Lewis's account is a good example of how delineating no difference between sentential truth and truth in the real world and not denoting all propositions taken into account in the abstractions can create further confusion. As Read (1995) summarises their view, they assumed that because of this (undenoted) contradictory background statement, the antecedent of the (b) counterfactual conditional is false, and so the counterfactual statement itself must always be true, because a false antecedent always makes a conditional statement true. This is in itself paradoxical, but they even added that if we add to the same counterfactual antecedent just the opposite of the initial consequent ('then no one would have', in our present example), the created counterfactual is also true, whereas it says exactly the opposite of the initial counterfactual statement. It is then concluded that for these reasons, the counterfactuals are not truth-functional.

However, if we differentiate between sentential truth and truth in the real world and denote the undenoted components, we can see, as we have already seen many times in this book, that the paradox can be removed, and we can make, once again, logic and everyday reasoning compatible with each other. In addition, we can make them compatible in such a way that even the simple, two-valued logic can be preserved with all of its benefits.

Let us briefly review the equivalent inferences in case of the (b) counterfactual conditional. When the antecedent is negated ('If Oswald would have killed Kennedy'), the background statement modifies to 'Oswald did not kill Kennedy'. Since this is in conflict with the background sentence of the initial statement, which said 'Oswald did kill Kennedy', the denial of the antecedent inference is not endorsed. We have already seen the same phenomenon at the end of Section 5.4, when in the case of 'if Aristotle wrote any dialogues, they have not survived', we did not endorse the denial of the antecedent inference, as it was against our everyday experience stating that non-written dialogues cannot survive.

Similarly, in the case of the affirmation of the consequent ('If someone would have killed Kennedy, Oswald would not have killed him'), we get the background statement that 'Oswald did kill Kennedy *because* someone else didn't'. This again opposes the original background sentence, since it gives a relation between Oswald and others that is just the opposite of what has been stated in the original sentence (the original sentence said that others would have killed Kennedy if Oswald wouldn't have); therefore, this inference is not endorsed, either. Finally, for the modus tollens ('If someone wouldn't have killed Kennedy, Oswald would have'), the background statement is modified once again ('Someone else killed Kennedy, not Oswald'); for this reason, this inference is also not endorsed.

In order to be able to endorse the equivalent inferences, it is sufficient to eliminate these background statements referring to the past. Since, as we discussed above, the counterfactual statements are actually clarifications or modifications of a relation in the past, we can do this by bringing back the complete conditional statement into the past. To do so, we can, for example, say that in the past, there was a conditional relationship that 'if Oswald doesn't kill Kennedy, someone else does'. This is obviously the same relationship that we have expressed above with a counterfactual, but in this case, we can already infer in the usual way, following, naturally, the equivalent inference pattern.

To sum up, in the case of counterfactual conditionals, we once again found undenoted components that are nonetheless taken into account when analysing the statements. These undenoted but at the same considered components are those 'facts' against which we formulate the counterfactual statements. When we denote these components, the phenomenon of the counterfactuals can easily be described, and in addition, can be described in such a way that we can preserve the simple, two-valued logic used throughout this book, as well as the basic equivalent interpretation of the conditional statement.

5.7 POSSIBLE WORLDS SEMANTICS

Stalnaker (1968, 1976) said that he introduced his approach primarily because of the counterfactuals (discussed in Section 5.6). It can also be seen that because of the paradox of the conditional statement (discussed in Section 5.3), because of the Raven paradox (discussed in Section 5.5) and because of the context effects in general that we have discussed, among others, in Sections 5.2 and 5.4. Stalnaker assumed that a solution to these problems is to assume that when we decide on the truth of a conditional statement, we add the antecedent to our actual stock of beliefs (in case of contradictory elements making the necessary minimal modifications on these beliefs), and we decide on this basis if the consequent is true or false.

Consequently, as Fisher (2008) explains it, the paradox of the conditional statement can be evaded because this approach presupposes adding an affirmed antecedent to our stock of beliefs; for this reason, the deduction from the negated antecedent does not make sense. Evans and Over (2004) say that with this approach, the paradox can be evaded by saying that in case of a negated antecedent, the truth of the 'if A then B' statement is optional. It depends on how plausibly we can imagine the B consequent when adding the A antecedent to our stock of beliefs. This is not affected, therefore, by a negated antecedent.

However, Stalnaker (1968), like principally everyone else, did not merely leave the context undenoted that he was clearly taking into account during the characterisations, and did not merely fail to differentiate between sentential truth and truth in the real world, but he actually generated an even larger set of undenoted context than usual for the purposes of his analyses. It was seen in the previous sections that denoting the context (and hence, among others, defining the equivalence inference pattern as the basic interpretation of the conditional statement) and differentiating sentential truth from the truth in the real world are not merely reasonable things to do, but actually enable us to offer a solution to the problems because of which Stalnaker (1968) introduced his theory.

Also, possible worlds semantics is already a relatively old approach. Consequently, the fact that it hasn't yet found its way into the psychological literature may suggest that this approach cannot be employed in an objective, empirical field. An implementation attempt was made by Rips and Marcus (1977), but their approach did not evolve into a general theory explaining the experimental results, and in general had very little influence on the field. Recently, Evans and Over (2004) investigated whether Stalnaker's approach can be linked to at least some of the experimental results of the psychological literature. For the abstract tasks, they did not reveal much correspondence, either, even though they suggest that Stalnaker's approach could possibly be used to describe performance on realistic, content-rich materials. However, they do not show experimental evidence for this, and even if they were to do so, the approach propagated in this book might be similarly able to describe this performance, being at the same time also capable of describing performance on abstract materials.

Finally, as with many other approaches, Stalnaker's approach does not seem compatible with the way the traditional interpretation of the conditional statement was actually defined in the antiquity.

5.8   THE RELATION TO PSYCHOLOGY

In sum, it is worth emphasising that if we take into account additional components during the abstractions, we should either denote them or ignore them completely. Whichever we choose, a great number of controversies surrounding the conditional statement will immediately disappear.

The fact that sentential truth and the truth in our experiences can be so easily mixed up with each other suggests that both of them can be depicted with the same logical apparatus; they simply have to be viewed as two separate systems being nonetheless in very close interaction with each other. Maybe even the 'real world' can be addressed as a third separate system, or it is simply everyday or common sense knowledge that a relatively large group of people believe to be true.

In everyday life, when we say that something is true or someone is right, it means that two or more of these logical systems—for example, the personal experiences of two different people, or the personal experiences of someone and what is stated in a book—are consistent with each other. When we observe apparent or real inconsistencies, we suspect that one of the two compared logical systems is mistaken or false.

Similarly, when we say in everyday life that someone is thinking logically, we mean by it that he or she interprets the explicit information—often by using his or her unstated or undenoted background knowledge—in a similar way as we do, and so the conclusions that he or she reaches are more or less consistent with our own conclusions. Also, arguing logically means to make explicit most of the information that we also believe is relevant in our background knowledge, as well as to establish similar connections between such explicit information as we would do on the basis of our background knowledge. Many conflicts arise by taking for granted that others have or should have the same background knowledge as we have.

From a cognitive point of view, it is also plausible to assume these three systems of truth: first, the logical inferential rules are the same for everyone; second, the everyday knowledge that builds up in one's mind, with the help of these rules—on the basis of one's different everyday experiences—is often different. This includes preferred coping strategies and of course is also shaped by temperamental differences. Third, all of this is continuously encountered with what is true either in the real world or in the opinions of others around us. Not taking into account, for the present, its emotional component, empathy, for example, in this respect is the ability to reconstruct someone else's unstated or partially stated background knowledge and infer on this basis with regard to an explicit situation.

In such a logic, again similar to the classical Greco-Roman logic and contrary to mathematical logic, categories and concepts also need to be addressed. Moreover, although the level of words appears adequate to distil the interpretation of the connectives, a psychologically motivated logical approach might be required to address a larger set of phenomena and to include emotions, motivations, intentions, memory and the rules of perception.

6 The recent probabilistic turn in the psychology of reasoning

6.1 TWO SIDES OF THE SAME COIN

Despite all of the above, in the psychological literature of the past 10 years, research has emphasised approaching the conditional statement in terms of probabilities *instead of* in terms of logic, and several authors (such as Evans & Over, 2004 and Evans, 2012), argue that the former can or should fully replace the latter.

In reality, however, both approaches are equally valid. In the 'If the snow is mixed with salt, it melts' statement that was analysed in Section 2.1, we can also ask about the probability of the occurrence of Q in the case of P. In such a case, we can recall previous cases in which the snow melted or did not melt after being salted, and we give our answers on this basis. It is obvious that counting the singular events this way is not in conflict with what we actually count, namely, the relation that when the snow is being salted (P), and, for example, the weather is not extremely cold (R), it melts (Q).

The difference arises because in the probabilistic approaches, the additional components (in this specific case, the event of extremely cold weather) are not denoted. Instead, the probability of Q in the case of P is calculated on the basis of the frequency of these undenoted components. This can clearly be seen, for example, in Evans and Over (2004, pp. 21-29) during their explanation of the Ramsey test (Ramsey, 1929/1990), the work of Stalnaker (1968) and the work of Lewis (1976). It can also be observed directly in Stalnaker (1968) as well, or in Oaksford and Chater (2003, pp. 364-365), who are also among the main proponents of the probabilistic approach. In fact, Ramsey (1929/1990), from whom this whole stream began, introduced his approach in such a way that the observed problem, which was the reason for introducing his interpretation, can also be handled with the approach advanced in this book.

Ramsey (1929/1990) said that we can imagine two people who have conflicting opinions regarding whether a P thing that one of them does triggers or does not trigger a Q event. These conflicting views can be expressed in two conflicting conditional statements. Then, as the traditional interpretation of the conditional goes, if the concerned person does not do the P thing, then both conditional statements will be true because their antecedents are false. Yet the two people could still have conflicting views on whether from P, Q follows or not. Ramsey said that in order to solve this issue, it must be assumed that these two people do not infer from the negated antecedent, but instead add the affirmed antecedent to their set of beliefs and infer on this basis the probability of the consequent.

According to the approach propagated here, however, the negated antecedent does not make the conditional statement universally true. It makes it true only if the consequent is also negated. This in itself refutes Ramsey's argumentation. In addition, Ramsey clearly did not differentiate between sentential truth and truth in the real world. Finally, he also left the context undenoted. This context is the source of the disagreement between the two people: their conflicting beliefs. These different beliefs can be found in two different systems, in the heads of these two separate people, and each can be valid within the given systems. So it is not paradoxical that there can be a disagreement between these two systems and that in one of these systems, from P, Q follows, and in the other system, it does not. Comparing these systems with regard to the actual question at stake, by trying to make explicit those propositions that are responsible for the conflicting beliefs, the discrepancy between them might be solved. This process is called discussion or debate. All in all, with these otherwise reasonable distinctions, Ramsey's example does not require us, as it is communicated, for example, by Evans and his colleagues, to abandon logic in the psychological field of reasoning and to introduce *solely* the probabilistic approach instead.

It is true that compared to traditional logic, where the undenoted components are not taken into account even in such an implicit way, the Ramsey-test related, probabilistic approaches give more plausible interpretations. However, as soon as we denote these undenoted components, logic instantly becomes a plausible alternative. In doing so, it can be seen that the logical and the probabilistic approaches are both valid. Quite simply, there are cases when we would like to know the frequencies and cases when we are interested in the inferential relations. It also happens that we have information for only one of these two possible analyses.

It is evident that in many of our opinions, we have only a certain degree of confidence. If, for example, we basically believe that the snow melts after being salted, but we also believe that sometimes it does not melt, then because of the stronger associative link, in case of the snow being salted, the belief that the snow will melt emerges as a more intensive belief and the belief that it does not melt as a weaker belief. If we then introspectively focus on the weaker belief that says the snow will not melt, this will bring to our working memory those components that provide the basis for this belief. From the point of view of logic, these are the unde-noted additional propositions mentioned several times in this book, and in this specific case, the 'extreme cold'.

Ramsey (1926/1990) was interested in objectively measuring such different degrees of beliefs, and he preferred the probabilistic approach. This preference was for two reasons. One is, of course, because he was a mathematician, and a mathematician naturally prefers, or at least knows better, the mathematical construct of probabilities instead of the construct of human sciences, associations. The other is that he believed that assum-ing different strengths of beliefs is not a viable option. However, he did not consider the strong associationist tradition in human sciences at all when he decided this, but was instead merely looking, very shortly, for some 'belief-feeling' (see Ramsey, 1926/1990, p. 65).

I believe that approaching the degrees of belief in terms of associative links can be a way to create a working abstract model of people's thinking processes. This is so even if we cannot calculate, at least at this level, the exact strength of these associations. In fact, as far as I can see, the proba-bilistic approaches are also unable to measure the exact level of the degrees of beliefs, except in such cases where these beliefs are explicitly based on numerical components.

Nonetheless, at least as an attempt, it can be accepted that mathemati-cians try to employ mathematical constructs in approaching everyday thinking procedures, assuming, of course, that this falls within their disci-pline. However, it is somewhat bizarre to see the way psychologists argue in support of such an approach. On one hand, they don't seem to address the strong associationist tradition of human sciences, and particularly that of psychology, when voting in favour of the probabilistic approach. In fact, as far as I know, they have not even investigated how, why and against what Ramsey introduced his approach. On the other hand, and even more importantly, when they advance this probabilistic approach *instead of* logic as such, they do not consider that ancient logic is at least as much a part of their own discipline as that of mathematics. They do not consider this to the degree that claiming that ancient logic is one of the historical precursors of psychology may sound even unnatural to the reader.

However, as already discussed in this book, ancient logic defined all logical abstractions currently studied in psychology, and these abstractions had nothing to do with mathematics. These abstractions belonged to human sciences, and the fact that they were also implemented into mathematics naturally does not mean that these old abstractions then became *exclusively* mathematical abstractions. What mathematicians added to these old abstractions has not yet proved to have any relevance to psychology. Perhaps this book also gave some evidence of this. We could cover the most intriguing questions relating to 'natural' or 'everyday' conditional inferences not only in psychology, but even in philosophy, without using anything other than good old scholastic logic.

We also discussed Stenning and van Lambalgen's (2008) approach in Sections 3.9 and 4.7.2, who are the only researchers currently using the tools of modern logic in explaining the findings of the psychological field of reasoning. I believe the approach advanced in this book outperforms their account in many respects, such as in explanatory power, predictive power, empirical support, simplicity and consistency.

6.2 EXPERIMENTAL COUNTER-ARGUMENTS AGAINST THE LOGICAL APPROACH

Despite all of the above, therefore, the proponents of the probabilistic approach in the psychological literature have a tendency to argue that the everyday interpretation of the conditional statement cannot be described in terms of logic. They refer to experiments that favour the probabilistic approach, but in these experiments, participants are directly asked about frequencies or degrees of certainty and/or are given frequency data (see Evans, Handley & Over, 2003; Oberauer & Wilhelm, 2003; Pfeifer, 2013), on which it is natural to receive frequency-based responses. In the experiments discussed in this book in Section 3, hardly any participants gave probabilistic responses, not even in the free-to-answer inference production task—which is normal, since they were not asked about probabilities.

Evans et al. (2003) or Oaksford and Chater (2003) also transform the logical truth values into probabilistic figures and compare them this way to their probabilistic accounts. However, these calculations do not currently take into account that in logic, the undenoted context and the undenoted additional components can be denoted, nor are the distorting effects of the experimental tasks discussed in Section 3 are addressed when making these transformations, such as the 'enumerative' interpretation in simple inference and truth table tasks or the avoidance of the selection of 'all' cards in the selection task. If no alternative or additional instances can emerge due to an explicit context that excludes them, such as in the equivalent ball-light problem discussed in Section 3.1, then the logical, biconditional responses immediately appear in inference production tasks at the high rate of 97% (Veszelka, 2007). That is, in such a case, logic, which basically has to deal with denoted components only, has nearly 100% predictive power.

So it is more interesting that Oaksford and Chater (1994), for example, could manage to describe the results of the abstract selection tasks without taking into account these demonstrable effects. Their analyses are based on various assumptions, such as the rarity assumption (Oaksford & Chater, 1994), which presupposes that participants treat P and Q as rare, but which has no considerable evidence from everyday life (even though a few instances are mentioned by Oaksford & Chater, 1998, p. 221 or Oaksford & Chater, 2007, pp. 207-208). With a similar assumption, they also assume that what is rare is more informative. Then, in abstract selection tasks, Oaksford and Chater (1994) have observed the P>Q>not-P>not-Q ordering in the selections. They argued that this selection frequency demonstrates the informativeness of the cards: the more a card is selected, the more it is informative. However, not only does this explanation run the risk of being circular, but the same, statistically not different P>Q>not-Q>not-P selection frequency occurred in the aforementioned ball-light problem when tested in the selection task (Veszelka, 2007). Yet because of the obvious equivalent relationship in this task, it is also obvious that every card is equally informative. This contradicts Oaksford and Chater's account.

In general, it can be observed that the deficient experimental results currently available in the field are generally employed to reject the logical approach. These include the abstract simple inference tasks and the difference between the frequency of the endorsed MP and MT inferences in these tasks (see Oaksford and Chater, 2003, 2010), mainly with implicit and sometimes with explicit negatives that, according to this book, follow from the 'enumerative' interpretation. The results with dichotomous negatives, showing the equivalent interpretation as the most characteristic answer, are not addressed in these accounts.

The arguments also include the results of the abstract truth table task (see Evans & Over, 2004, p. 36), but only with implicit and sometimes with explicit negatives, without addressing the results with dichotomous negatives that directly show, once again, equivalent inferences as the most characteristic answers. The arguments also include the abstract selection task (Evans & Over, 2004, chapter 5; Oaksford & Chater, 2003) and the matching bias (Evans & Over, 2004, chapter 3), but never abstract inference production tasks that, once again, show predominant equivalent inferences with all three types of negatives.

As shown in Table 2, many of the relevant results were, in fact, not even available until 2007, and even after 2007, as far as I know, the missing data were available only in my paper written in Hungarian, which naturally had no influence on the English language literature. As seen in Section 3, running these missing experiments and some others reveals a radically different picture of people's everyday inferences. They actually show that people basically interpret the conditional statement as an equivalent relation.

Finally, Evans and Over (2004) also refer to the allegedly non-logical facilitation in thematic selection tasks (chapters 3 and 6) as proof against logic, but we have seen in Section 3 that on one hand, this facilitation effect can also be approached in terms of logic, and on the other hand, the assumption of such non-logical facilitations is not normatively valid.

6.3 THEORETICAL COUNTER-ARGUMENTS AGAINST THE LOGICAL APPROACH

With regard now to the theoretical counter-arguments against the logical approach, a central argument in the literature is the interpretation of the conditional statement as prescribed in propositional logic (see, for example, Edgington, 2003, 2007; Evans & Over, 2004). The present book also suggests that this interpretation is indeed not suitable to describe the results. However, after fixing this principally ancient abstraction, the experimental results can be quite effectively explained.

The possibility of the logical description is also questioned by arguing against its truth-functional nature, mentioning the paradox of the conditional statement as the main example (see Stalnaker, 1968; Edgington, 2003, 2007, 2008; Evans & Over, 2004, pp. 19-20; Manktelow, 2012, p. 60). However, as seen in Section 5.3, the updated interpretation of the conditional statement and the denotation of the undenoted components resolve this paradox and allow the retention of the simplest two-valued, truth functional logic.

Sometimes, instances or contexts taken into account during the characterisations but left undenoted are explicitly mentioned as distorting and hence refuting the logical abstractions (see Edgington, 2003, 2007; Evans & Over, 2004, pp. 20-22; the 'beetle' example on pages 8-9 of Oaksford & Chater, 2010). Yet by denoting these components, the possibility of the logical interpretation is immediately restored.

Stalnaker (1968), Evans and Over (2004, pp. 146-147) and Oaksford and Chater (2010, p. 8) also mention Hempel's paradox as an example, a paradox that we have discussed in Section 5.5.

The defeasible nature of everyday inferences is also an argument against the logical approach (see Evans & Over, 2004, p. 92), but as seen in Section 2.3 of this book with regard to pragmatic inferences and in Sections 2.3 and 5.1 with regard to non-monotonic logics, this does not constitute a viable argument against it.

Evans and Over (2004, pp. 93-95) also mention the belief bias first observed by Wilkins (1928), in which people evaluate logical inferences on the basis of their believability, that is, on the basis of taking into account their additional thoughts on the subject matter. I believe that denoting these undenoted but at the same time considered components is as viable a way as is leaving them undenoted and interpreting them as some kind of logically unidentifiable 'bias'.

Following the established practice in the literature, Evans and Over (2004, chapter 6) also interpret the influence of undenoted alternative antecedents on the conditional statement as pragmatic, and as such, as being in conflict with logic. It was, however, seen throughout this book, particularly in Sections 2.1 and 2.2, that the effect of these undenoted alternative antecedents is so logical that it is deeply and inseparably rooted in the ancient abstraction of the conditional statement.

The experimental and theoretical arguments discussed in these last three sections are all considered to be major arguments against the logical interpretation. Consequently, what we have already seen through this book could also be seen here from a different direction: the predominant arguments and experimental results against the logical interpretation in the psychological field of reasoning not only allow us to maintain such an interpretation, but after running some additional experiments and making some theoretical considerations, they even offer support for it.

7 Closing remarks

In this book, we have discussed the interpretation of the conditional statement. After fixing a clearly identifiable, ancient abstraction error, we can immediately resolve several current psychological and philosophical problems. We can quite effectively systematise the results of the main psychological experimental tasks and can expand all of this into a unified framework which explains the paradox of the conditional statement, the Raven paradox, the counterfactuals, the pragmatic conditional inferences, the syllogisms or the basic effects of context. The approach presented here can also be made compatible with today's popular probabilistic accounts of the interpretation of the conditional statement.

This approach is rather simple, so many might believe it is just too simplistic. However, making something more complicated does not necessary make it correct. Something can be complicated simply because it is made without due consideration or because it is based on mistakes. We have also seen that despite its simplicity, the approach suggested here has a rather strong explanatory power. In addition to this, exactly because of its simplicity, a further benefit of this approach is that possibly, it could be easily programmed into a computer and adapted to explain further questions relating to everyday thinking or other psychological phenomena, more easily than, for example, non-monotonic logics created in principle for the same purposes. In fact, this account gives a good explanation of why traditional and modern forms of logic have been unsuccessful in describing 'natural' intelligence, and hence, in paving a possible way for creating 'artificial' intelligence.

On the other hand, as far as psychology is concerned, this account provides an exact, abstract standpoint from which to describe people's inferences. In Section 5.8, we noted several points through which this approach connects immediately to more widely considered psychological phenomena. We have also seen that many of the experiments reported in this book directly contradict the current psychological theories. Most importantly, these theories are based on experimental observations, in some cases lasting across several decades, which have no solid foundations due to unsystematic research.

In addition, regardless of whether we are discussing logical or psychological theories, these are not consistent with how the conditional statement was actually abstracted 2,400 years ago. Some researchers point out—to me, at least—that we need not be concerned with the history of the conditional statement. However, it is not difficult to realise that if a central abstraction error has been made that influences even today's systems, then this mistake has to be fixed. Moreover, it must be carefully examined how this mistake influenced those systems that are, in fact, partially based on this mistake. Finally, the development of those disciplines are also of interest that are reflective in part of these mistaken systems and their relative ineffectiveness. For instance, psychology was born and developed so that even before it appeared, logic was already found, in fact, to be unable to describe human inferences. Otherwise, both logic and psychology would have developed very differently.

Logical artificial intelligence, a branch of artificial intelligence, is a similar example that focuses, in several respects, on everyday reasoning and on its logical description. However, due to the historical reasons illustrated in this book, researchers in this field do not look beyond mathematical logic when thinking about logic, and they also do not consider the relevant psychological literature. Instead, they try to find out by themselves how the mind works, even though this has a long tradition both in psychology and in the philosophy of mind.

A further example of the problems caused by the lack of historical perspective, on the other hand, is how logic is currently treated in psychology. As explained in this book, the main connectives of logic, including the conditional statement and syllogisms in general, were abstracted in a philosophical, linguistic, psychological context instead of a mathematical one. Consequently, these abstractions are at least as closely related to linguistics or to psychology as they are to mathematics. Hence, when psychologists, with a degree of reluctance against logic, are searching 'psychological' theories to explain everyday logical inferences *instead of* 'logical' theories, they have a degree of reluctance against their own historical roots and want to differentiate themselves from these very roots. Disconnecting from our own roots is never beneficial. As shown in this book, doing so makes it impossible to fix the mistakes of the past.

It is an interesting phenomenon that people who do not understand the long-term historical perspective of going back to the roots of the problem to check where things first went wrong are often very sensitive to a short-term historical perspective. For example, in order to accept this present study for peer review in scientific journals, journal editors expected 10- to 30-year-old studies to be carefully discussed, yet when a considerable amount of such studies were then processed, they pointed out that the material was too long and so could not be peer reviewed. This is a Catch-22, but at least no one can say that today's intensive academic research on the topic has no applied side.

I believe the present book clearly evidences that a historical approach going beyond the beginning of the 20th century can be beneficial. This study also provides a good example of how research questions can often be very simple at the beginning; the successive mistakes, lies becoming dogmas, classifications and extensive studies made without due considerations, etc. can all vastly contribute to make a question complicated and extensive. In this book, the reader can see that after fixing the abstraction error, we immediately achieve a logic which is much more flexible, much more in line with everyday life and inseparably connected to psychology.

We have also seen in Sections 4.8 and 5.1 that this fixed interpretation of the conditional statement creates connections for embedding learning processes into the basic abstractions of logic. In fact, the new abstraction of the conditional statement makes it even necessary to establish such a connection. I am confident that through this connection, we can approach even such phenomena as humour, motivation, emotions and intuition in terms of logic. I believe these come from the very same source. I have a very simple model for this, but it will not be discussed in this book. Connecting these components together can lead us to create a thinking machine, and of course, understanding thinking processes can be useful for psychology in itself.

Nowadays, there is a growing interest among logicians to describe psychological processes in terms of logic, but most of them expect to have a breakthrough without being willing to make changes to their basic assumptions and dogmas. Earlier, the situation was the same with cognitive psychology as well. This psychological research paradigm, which, about

50 years after the birth of 'scientific psychology', that is, after the birth of the behaviourist paradigm, finally allowed for psychologists, in fact, to open philosophical books, and which—perhaps because of feeling in consequence threatened by logic and philosophy—turned since then considerably towards neurology, was also receptive to logic only to a very limited degree. In the same way, modern logic is not really receptive to what happened before the beginning of the 19th-20th centuries, before the mathematicalisation of logic. However, things did happen before behaviourism and before the mathematicalisation of logic.

In this book, many components of the literature were left unaddressed. No detailed discussion was given about today's psychological, linguistic and philosophical literature. With regard to the latter, a reason to leave these studies mainly unaddressed was that as far as I know, these have not yet been connected to the empirical results of the psychological field. Grice's everyday implicatures and the assumption of the existence of pragmatic inferences are exceptions. These frequently reappear in the experimental literature as well and have therefore been briefly discussed in Sections 2.3, 4.7.2 and 5.4.

Similarly, I also addressed the research of Evans and Over (2004), who currently attempt to adapt today's popular, probabilistic, Ramsey-test-related philosophical interpretation of the conditional statement to the experimental results. We have seen in Sections 5.7 and 6 that from the philosophical side, these approaches, as with many others, disregard the fundamental principle of denoting the propositions taken into account during the abstractions. From the experimental side, on the other hand, it was also shown in Sections 3 and 6 that like many other researchers, Evans and Over also attempt to demonstrate comprehensive components on the basis of incomplete and misleading experimental results, often even making further selections from the results currently available to them.

For example, Cheng et al. (1986) presented results almost 30 years ago showing that a thematic selection task with a definitely equivalent relationship conceals the equivalent inferences and produces instead the selection of P and Q values. This has never been considered by the researchers in the field, including Evans and Over (2004), when building their non-logical theories on the bizarre selection of the same P and Q values observed in the abstract selection task. The experiments presented in this book show that by filling some of the fundamental experimental gaps, we receive a completely different overall picture about people's conditional inferences, and that this picture can immediately be employed to address several current logico-philosophical questions.

Of course, there is a chance, as always, that what is stated in this book is a mistake. But it is at least a systematic mistake that can be developed further or confidently rejected with additional systematic research. Still, there seemed to be clear opposition to considering these results in the peer-reviewed literature. This was my experience with multiple journals and editors, and my experience was often very devastating. Even in less devastating cases, I was, for example, told that the selection task was already overstudied, so this research is of no interest. However, labelling the research on the selection task undesirable prevents someone from actually explaining why this task produces the results it does and from presenting a simple approach, as seen in this book.

As a perhaps unintended effect of this attitude, the ever-growing, unsystematic and already unprocessably large psychological literature defends psychology from logic breaking in, without the need to present valid arguments and well-established experimental data against it. In theory, such a field would also allow some to control without much scientific basis what is let in and what must stay out. Another possible component can be that keeping a field obscure may allow for the publication of more studies because it is simpler to add deficient papers to an inconsistent literature than actually resolving problems and then turning toward resolving new problems. I have no better idea.

On the other side, logicians have similarly buried the abstraction error in logic beyond the realm of contemporary research. They claim that formal, mathematical logics are much more developed than ancient logic, and particularly, that these logics have been created independently of it. The fact that the same abstraction error can be found both in scholastic logic and in the predominant mathematical logic of the 20th century, propositional logic, as discussed in Section 2.2, clearly challenges this latter claim. Perhaps what has been discussed in this book also challenges, to an extent, the former. However, on the basis of these claims, it is considered unscientific with regard to today's scientific problems to go back to the 'entirely insignificant' (Tarski, 1946/1995, p. 19) scholastic logic. Perhaps coincidentally, the historical perspective in logic is also frequently seen as somewhat unnecessary and unscientific.

As a consequence, Burgess (2009, p. 1), for example, writes that since the abstraction of the conditional statement was made for analysing arguments in mathematics, it's not a surprise that it has to be adjusted when adapted to questions outside of mathematics. We have seen in this book that the classical abstraction of the conditional statement had nothing to do with mathematics. It can be traced back to Aristotle (384-322 BC) (1928) or, for example, to Boethius (480-524 or 525 AD) (before 522/1988) or Avicenna (980-1038 AD) (1955), and their example sentences were by no means mathematical sentences.

This is not an isolated example. A peer reviewer from a mathematically oriented journal pointed out against my account, in this case, with regard to syllogisms, that 'to assert that «All A are B» is equivalent to «All B are A» flies in the face of over two thousand years of mathematics.' Here again, it is sufficient to open a book on syllogisms, particularly one which is more than 100-200 years old, to see that the abstraction of syllogisms had nothing to do with mathematics. In fact, we have already seen the same argument in the citation from Aristotle in Section 2.1. The reader can easily verify whether this citation has anything to do with mathematics. This reviewer had also a very short argument against taking into account and critically thinking over how the syllogisms were actually abstracted, on one hand, and against evaluating the relevant experimental data in an attempt to provide an abstract framework to characterise human (and probably, of course, animal) inferences, on the other hand. The reviewer said that 'logic is not democratic'. It is unclear how this is so.

Sometimes I replied to the reviews that I received from the philosophical, logical and psychological journals, and this review was also among them. The editor thanked me for my interest in the journal and said that the publication selected the reviewers on the basis of their expertise. He said that I could resubmit my paper if I rewrote it on the basis of the reviews received. Unfortunately, it was impossible to rewrite my paper on this basis. As such, again perhaps accidentally, the logico-philosophical literature has grown extensive on a foundation that defends logic from psychology breaking in.

In both disciplines, these procedures rule out the possibility of an organic investigation of logical truth and necessity or that of the relation between psychology and logic, making it difficult to see the real origins of these concepts and these disciplines, to do research on them and, most importantly, to share the obtained results. As a consequence, logical truth and necessity, or the relation between psychology and logic, have been studied in the past 100 years on grounds that are considerably misleading.

A clear example of this can be seen in Evans (2012), who, although a leading researcher in the psychological field of reasoning from the very beginning, believes that the field was founded as a reply to a general logicist approach in psychology, where the constructions of propositional logic were accepted as a valid tool to describe everyday (logical) inferences.

In reality, disregarding sporadic deviations, such as that of Inhelder and Piaget (1958), who were frequently cited by Evans, there was no such approach in psychology. Throughout the 19th and early 20th centuries, there was a prolonged debate within philosophy regarding the logistic and psychologistic approaches of knowledge (epistemology). This debate can be traced back to the time at which Kant separated logic and empirical psychology (see Hatfield, 2013, p. 176). Psychology has since been hostile towards logic and vice versa. Logic threatened the foundation—and hence, the position—of psychology, and psychology threatened those of logic.

The debate also addressed approaching logic in terms of psychology, which is called 'logical psychologism' or—from the perspective of logicians—simply 'psychologism'. Within the movement, it is assumed that logic is compatible with psychology or that it is even a part of psychology. The present book can therefore be allocated to the category 'psychologism' by logicians while being simultaneously labelled 'logicism' by psychologists. Kusch (1995, 2014) offers a robust and detailed summary of this debate, with a particular focus on the various arguments that were brought forward against logical psychologism; I believe the arguments and experimental results presented in this book directly refute most of these earlier arguments.

Nonetheless, both logicism and psychologism significantly contributed to the development of their fields. The logicist approach of philosophy, for instance, created analytic philosophy, a 20th century movement that is still dominant in philosophy today, while the empirical approach of psychology created both behaviourism and a very strong experimental tradition that continues to be upheld. At the same time, however, logical psychologism has disappeared, and it is difficult even to remember its proponents. Any sign of logical psychologism continues to be heavily attacked both by psychologists, the successors of behaviourists, and by logicians, the successors of the logicists, from the beginning of the 20th century.

Maybe this explains why the research presented in this book has always been rejected without presenting any real counterarguments against it, and often without even presenting any arguments at all. The journal editors perhaps believed that this approach was already refuted by both psychologists and logicians 100 years ago, and so it is pointless to reopen this question for debate. Consequently, they mostly rejected my research without even a formal review. This is, however, only a guess, as they never told me that. I have such guesses because I still believe science is about arguments, so when I lack these arguments, I try to figure them out myself.

My argument for logical psychologism is that the logical psychologism of the beginning of the 20th century was too speculative. Even if I find many of the arguments in favour of logical psychologism to be more convincing than the arguments in favour of the logicist approach, the proponents of psychologism did not know how to connect logic and psychology at the most elementary level. Consequently, they couldn't create a psychological logic that could be used for the purposes of psychology, whereas mathematical logic was successfully and intensively advanced both in mathematics and philosophy. In addition, psychologists were not even very interested in logical psychologism, as the mainstream of psychologist epistemology soon turned towards human experimentation and for several decades they labelled philosophical (including logical) speculations as not fitting into the strictly empirical foundations of 'scientific' psychology. However, in contrast to the speculative psychological logic of the beginning of the 20th century, the psychologism presented in this book is very straightforward. First, it suggests that the logical constructs of the conditional statement and the universal affirmative statement, which logicists interpreted as being 'pure', 'eternally' or 'universally' true, were in fact the result of fallible, partly mistaken judgements of ancient logicians. Second, it was demonstrated with—hopefully—rigorous psychological experiments that when these normative rules are fixed, they can also be applied fairly well as descriptive rules for predicting or explaining people's actual inferences. Third, this approach is deeply and organically rooted in the history of logic. Actually, it goes back to the very foundations of logic: it organically emerges from logic by pointing out the obvious and widespread error of failing to consider all propositions during the logical characterisations. As this book reveals, this principle is largely neglected in modern logic, despite the fact that it is even more fundamental than the characterisation of logical connectives. Consequently, it allows us to fix the error committed in the characterisation of one of the connectives, that of the conditional statement.

Nonetheless, turning back to traditional logic and psychology, as discussed in the Introduction, there is a twist in using propositional logic as a normative background in psychology, as this approach has its origins precisely in the big opponent of psychology, logicism. Logicists assumed that the deviations from propositional logic in everyday life reveal linguistic or psychological components. So, whereas they rejected the idea of approaching psychological phenomena in terms of logic when this was done by logical psychologists, it must be noted that they were not so decisive against this when psychological phenomena were approached in terms of their own logic, propositional logic, and in terms of their own assumptions.

In either way, one hundred years ago, empirical psychologists therefore revolutionised thinking about psychology, and logicists revolutionised thinking about logic as well as mathematics and philosophy. Since logicists (analytic philosophers) viewed language as a tool to study thinking, their approach provided a great impetus to the philosophy of language. The philosophy of language then naturally made its way to linguistics, and then through psycholinguistics, the initially logicist methodology was finally implemented into the big opponent, psychology, by Peter Wason. He was the founder of the psychological field of reasoning as we know it today, as well as the tutor of Johnson-Laird, the main proponent of the mental models theory briefly discussed in Section 4.7.1, and of Evans.

In fact, Evans also revealed many psychological components, various biases and heuristics on the basis of what he observed in light of the normative background of propositional logic. For example, he coined, in most of the cases precisely with regard to the conditional statement, matching bias (see Evans, 1972), anti-matching bias (Evans, Ellis & Newstead, 1996), conclusion bias (Pollard & Evans, 1980), negative conclusion bias (see Evans, 1995), post-reasoning conclusion filter (see Evans, Clibbens & Rood, 1995, p. 663), caution effect (Pollard & Evans, 1980; Evans et al., 1995, p. 663), affirmative premise bias (see Pollard & Evans, 1980; Evans, 1993; Evans et al., 1995) or affirmative premise effect (Evans & Handley, 1999), negative premise effect (Evans & Handley, 1999), if and not-heuristic (see Evans, 1989; Evans et al., 1996), matching heuristic (Evans,

Legrenzi & Girotto, 1999, p. 189), double negation effect (see Evans et al., 1995, p. 663), implicit negation effect (Evans & Handley, 1999), 'double hurdle' theory (Evans & Handley, 1999), general positivity bias (Evans, 1995) and belief bias (see Evans & Over, 1997, p. 17). As far as I know, most of these constructs never made their way into the common knowledge in the field, but the reasons for this cannot be investigated here.

Also, on the basis of the arguably deceptive and deficient experimental results, many of which have been discussed in this book, but still following propositional logic as a normative reference point, Evans posited various so-called dual process theories (see Evans, 1989; Evans & Over, 2004; Evans, 2012). These assumed a heuristic phase, among others, on the basis of the deficient abstract task results, and a rational phase, among others, on the basis of the normatively misinterpreted easy-to-resolve thematic selection task results. However, the fact that psychology in general was not accepting logic as a normative tool resulted in the field being largely separated from the mainstream.

Evans (2012) now proposes a 'new paradigm', leaving behind logic as a normative background and aiming to provide a descriptive account of everyday reasoning without the need to define a normative reference point. He also expects that in this way, the field could be better integrated into the mainstream of psychology.

On the basis of the above considerations, this expectation might be valid. Also, the attempt after almost 50 years to give at least a descriptive account of people's actual inferences can also be welcomed, even though if logic is not of interest anymore, it is unclear what kind of inferences Evans aims to study and for what purposes. I remember in elementary school, I once was asked to write about a 'brick'. Since I was not instructed in which sense I should write about the brick and for what purpose, that task, if properly performed, could last eternally. I believe simply studying 'inferences' is somewhat the same.

In any case, Evans (2012) suggests that there are actually reasons for leaving behind logic which, according to this book, cannot be corroborated. It was seen that after running some basic experiments that have been missing for several decades, the results show that logic, even though in an updated form, actually performs very well as a descriptive tool of people's everyday conditional inferences. It was also shown that by having a look at how the conditional statement was abstracted in the antiquity, people's performance can even be normatively justified. I hope I also managed to give some examples in this book to show that the conditional statement can indeed be seen as the entry door to the abstraction of more complex everyday reasoning, and ultimately, to the abstraction of more complex psychological phenomena.

I believe the problems faced by logic and psychology, particularly with regard to 'natural' or 'everyday' inferences, can be solved in only one way: by carefully investigating and evaluating the pasts of these disciplines, that is, the previous steps that have led to today's complex situation, by systematic and rigorous empirical testing and by building consistent theories.

There is, however, another way. It does not resolve many of the questions posed by this fragmented, interdisciplinary field, but it allows the intensive study of reasoning to continue and even to make some achievements, without revealing that the king lacks some of his clothes: It's the probabilistic approach, which leaves the foundations of both psychology and modern logic untouched, particularly that of the latter, and thus can be accepted by the proponents of both disciplines.

Perhaps this explains why this approach, in various forms, is gaining momentum. It became quite popular in philosophy as early as in the 1970s, perhaps because it allowed one to study natural logical reasoning without threatening mathematics, and now, efforts are being made to implement it into psychology as well.

The procedure was already once successful, namely, when Peter Wason implemented the former logicist paradigm of the 1920s into psychology in the 1960s. Evans (2012) seems enthusiastic about this 'new paradigm in reasoning', about dropping logic as a reference point and hence, making connections to a great plethora of psychological concepts and results from other psychological fields. However, an alternative approach could be, I must note, to first make the basic experimental data complete and consistent.

Either way, instead of giving a detailed review in this book of this psychological and logico-philosophical literature, I tried to collect together the most significant questions and the most predominant experimental tasks. Consequently, this book suggested that the basic interpretation of the conditional statement is the equivalence, and that a major problem complicating the field of everyday or natural reasoning, both in philosophical logic and in psychology, is that researchers simply do not denote all instances that they take into account during the logical characterisations.

Several examples have been shown in this book of how to find this basic equivalent interpretation and those components that are undenoted but that are at the same time still taken into account. The reader will see that after becoming familiar with it, this procedure can immediately be employed in the case of many studies and sample sentences not directly mentioned in this book.

On the other hand, in cases when the basic equivalent inferences and the role of the undenoted context are not immediately evident, or the basic equivalent inferences seem to be distorted for some reason, further observations can be made on how the conditional statement or logic functions in everyday life, or, if the reader wishes, in real life. An example of such a starting point is that, as we have seen at the end of Section 5.4 and in Section 5.6, some inferences are not endorsed when everyday knowledge or personal experiences are in conflict with them. Among others, this is also a way to approach more complex thinking processes and to describe them in terms of logic.

On the basis of this observation, made on a very elementary level in the aforementioned sections, it can be raised, for example, that the same happens when we read selectively or have 'no ear to hear' content that does not match with our beliefs. Sometimes, this is a positive phenomenon, because maybe we are right, and then it is unnecessary to waste time and energy trying to understand an alternative approach. It's always frustrating to deal with a problem without any really useful outcome, just spending time to reveal where the possibly complicated alternative approach actually goes wrong. With the term 'frustration', we have also touched here the emotional component of logic, a component that was not addressed in this book but can be elaborated upon further. The point I would like to make here is that it can also be the case, however, that by assuming the burden of giving room to new ideas (the burden of placing new logical relations into our background knowledge), we can discover that our own everyday, personal or scientific experience (whatever we call it) requires modification or can be expanded further. It is for the reader to decide with regard to this book which one was the case.

8 Literature

Adams, E. W. (1970). Subjunctive and indicative conditionals. *Foundations of Language, 6(1)*, 89-94.

Andrews, A. D. (1993). Mental models and tableau logic. *Behavioral and Brain Sciences, 16*, 334.

Aristotle (1928). De sophisticis elenchis. In: W. D. Ross. (ed), *The works of Aristotle*, Oxford: Oxford University Press.

Avicenna (1955). *Le livre de science I. Logic, métaphisique.* (M. Achena & H. Massé Trans.) Paris: Les Belles Lettres.

Barouillet, P., & Lecas J. F. (1998). How can mental models theory account for content effects in conditional reasoning? A developmental perspective. *Cognition, 67*, 209-253.

Blanché, R. (1970). *La logique et son histoire d'Aristote à Russell.* Paris: Librairie Armand Colin.

Boethius (before 522/1988). *In Ciceronis Topica.* Ithaca and London: Cornell University Press.

Brennan J. G. (1961). *A handbook of logic.* Second edition. New York: Harper and Row.

Burgess, J. P. (2009). *Philosophical logic.* Princeton, NJ: Princeton University Press.

Byrne, R. M. J. (1989). Suppressing valid inferences with conditionals. *Cognition, 31*, 61-83.

Byrne R. M. J., Espino, O., & Santamaria, C. (1999). Counterexamples and the suppression of inferences. *Journal of Memory & Language, 40*, 347-373.

Byrne, R. M. J. & Tasso, A. (1999). Deductive reasoning with factual, possible, and counterfactual conditionals. *Memory & Cognition, 27*, 726-740.

Chapman, L. J. & Chapman, J. P. (1959). Atmosphere effect re-examined. *Journal of Experimental Psychology, 58(3)*, 220-226.

Chater, N., & Oaksford, M. (1999). The probability heuristics model of syllogistic reasoning. *Cognitive Psychology, 38*, 191-258.

Cheng, P. W., & Holyoak, K. J. (1985). Pragmatic reasoning schemas. *Cognitive Psychology, 17*, 391-416.

Cheng, P. W., Holyoak, K. J., Nisbett, R. E., & Oliver, L. M. (1986). Pragmatic versus syntactic approaches to training deductive reasoning. *Cognitive Psychology 18*, 293-328.

Copeland, D. E. (2006). Theories of categorical reasoning and extended syllogisms. *Thinking & Reasoning 12(4)*, 379-412.

Copi, I. M. (1982). *Introduction to logic.* New York: Macmillan.

Copi, I. M., & Cohen, C. (1998). *Introduction to logic.* Tenth edition. Upper Saddle River, NJ: Prentice-Hall.

Cosmides, L. (1989). The logic of social exchange: Has natural selection shaped how humans reason? Studies with the Wason selection task. *Cognition 31*, 187- 316.

Cummins, D. D., Lubart, T., Alksnis, O., & Rist, R. (1991). Conditional reasoning and causation. *Memory & Cognition, 19(3)*, 274-282.

Dickstein, L. S. (1978). The effect of figure on syllogistic reasoning. *Memory & Cognition, 6(1)*, 76-83.

Douven, I., & Verbrugge, S. (2010). The Adams family. *Cognition, 117,* 302-318.

Edgington, D. (2003). What if? Questions about conditionals. *Mind and Language, 18(4)*, 380-401.

Edgington, D. (2007). On Conditionals. In D. M. Gabbay, & F. Guenthner (eds*),* *On conditionals. Handbook of philosophical logic, Vol 14*, 2nd edition, (pp. 127-221), Dordrecht: Springer.

Edgington, D. (2008). Conditionals. In E. N. Zalta (ed), *The Stanford Encyclopedia of Philosophy (Winter 2008 Edition)*, URL: http://plato.stanford.edu/archives/win2008/entries/conditionals/

Eidens, H. (1929). Experimentelle Untersuchungen über den Denkverlauf bei unmittelbaren Folgerungen. *Archiv für die Gesamte Psychologie, 71*, 1-66.

Euler, L. (1768-1772/1842). *Lettres de L. Euler à une princesse d'Allemagne sur divers sujets de physique et de philosophie*. Paris: L. Hachette.

Evans, J. St. B. T. (1972). Interpretation and matching bias in a reasoning task. *Quarterly Journal of Experimental Psychology, 24*, 193-199.

Evans, J. St. B. T. (1989). *Bias in human reasoning: Causes and consequences*. Howe, UK: Lawrence Erlbaum.

Evans, J. St. B. T. (1991). Theories of human reasoning: The fragmented state of the art. *Theory and Psychology, 1*, 83-105.

Evans, J. St. B. T. (1993). The mental model theory of conditional reasoning: critical appraisal and revision. *Cognition, 48*, 1-20.

Evans, J. St. B. T. (1995). Relevance and Reasoning. In S. E. Newstead, & J. St. B. T. Evans (eds), *Perspectives on thinking and reasoning: Essays in honour of Peter Wason* (pp. 147-171). Hove, UK: Lawrence Erlbaum Associates Ltd.

Evans, J. St. B. T. (1996). Deciding before you think: Relevance and reasoning in the selection task. *British Journal of Psychology 87(2)*, 223-240.

Evans, J. St. B. T. (1998). Matching bias in conditional reasoning: Do we understand it after 25 years? *Thinking and Reasoning, 4*, 45-82.

Evans, J. St. B. T. (2012). Questions and challenges for the new psychology of reasoning. *Thinking & Reasoning, 18(1)*, 5-31.

Evans, J. St. B. T., & Ball, L. J. (2010). Do people reason on the Wason selection task? A new look at the data of Ball et al. (2003). *Quarterly Journal of Experimental Psychology, 63(3), 434-441.*

Evans, J. St. B. T., Clibbens, J., & Rood, B. (1995). Bias in conditional Inference: Implications for mental models and mental logic. *Quarterly journal of Experimental Psychology, 48A*, 644-670.

Evans, J. St. B. T., Clibbens, J., & Rood, B. (1996). The role of implicit and explicit negation in conditional reasoning bias. *Journal of Memory & Language 35(3)*, 392-409.

Evans, J. St. B. T., Ellis, C. E., & Newstead, S. E. (1996). On the mental representation of conditional sentences. *Quarterly Journal of Experimental Psychology, 49A,* 1086-1114.

Evans, J. St. B. T., & Handley, S. J. (1999). The role of negation in conditional inference. *Quarterly Journal of Experimental Psychology, 52A,* 739-769.

Evans, J. St. B. T., Handley, S. J., & Over, D. E. (2003). Conditionals and conditional probability. *Journal of Experimental Psychology: Learning, Memory, and Cognition, 29(2),* 321-335.

Evans, J. St. B. T., Legrenzi, P., & Girotto, V. (1999). The influence of linguistic form on reasoning: The case of matching bias. *Quarterly Journal of Experimental Psychology, 52A,* 185-216.

Evans, J. St. B. T., & Lynch, J. S. (1973). Matching bias in the selection task. *British Journal of Psychology, 64,* 391-397.

Evans, J. St. B. T., Newstead, S. E, & Byrne, R. M. J. (1993). *Human reasoning: The psychology of deduction.* Hove, UK: Lawrence Erlbaum Associates Ltd.

Evans, J. St. B. T., & Over, D. E. (1996). *Rationality and reasoning: The problem of deductive competence.* Hove, UK: Psychology Press.

Evans, J. St. B. T., & Over, D. E. (1997). Rationality in reasoning: The problem of deductive competence. *Cahiers de Psychologie Cognitive/ Current Psychology of Cognition, 16 (1-2),* 3-38.

Evans, J. St. B. T., & Over, D. E. (2004). *If.* Oxford: Oxford University Press

Fiddick, L., & Erlich, N. (2010). Giving it all away: altruism and answers to the Wason selection task. *Evolution and Human Behavior, 31(2),* 131-140.

Fillenbaum, S. (1974). Information amplified: memory for counterfactual conditionals. *Journal of Experimental Psychology, 102,* 44-49.

Fisher, J. (2008). *On the philosophy of logic.* Belmont, CA: Wadsworth, Cengage Learning.

Frege, G. (1879). *Begriffsschrift: eine der arithmetischen nachgebildete Formelsprache des reinen Denkens.* Halle.

Frege, G. (1918-19/1984). Logical investigations. In B. McGuinness (ed), *Collected papers on mathematics, logic, and philosophy* (pp. 351-407). Oxford: Basil Blackwell.

Gál, G. (1979). Paul of Venice, *Logica Magna, II, 6: Tractatus de veritate et falsitate propositionis et Tractatus de significato propositionis.* Edited with notes on the sources by Francesco del Punta, translated into English with explanatory notes by Marilyn McCord Adams. (Classical and Medieval Logic Texts, 1.) Oxford, England, and New York: Oxford University Press, for the British Academy, 1978. Pp. xvi, 294. $37.50.; Boethius, *De topicis differentiis.* Translated, with notes and essays on the text, by Eleonore Stump. Ithaca, N.Y., and London: Cornell University Press, 1978. Pp. 288. $18.50., *Speculum 54(3),* 614-617.

Geis, M. L, & Zwicky, A. M. (1971). On invited inferences. *Linguistic Inquiry, 2,* 561-566.

George, C. (1992). Rules of inference in the interpretation of the conditional connective. *Cahiers de Psychologie Cognitive/ Current Psychology of Cognition, 12(2),* 115-139.

Grice, P, (1975). Logic and conversation. In P. Cole, & J. L. Morgan (eds), *Syntax and semantics, Vol 3.: Speech Acts* (pp. 41-58). New York: Academic press.

Griggs, R. A., & Cox, J. R. (1982). The elusive thematic-materials effect in Wason's selection task. *British Journal of Psychology, 73,* 407-420.

Hardman, D. (1998). Does reasoning occur on the selection task? A comparison of relevance-based theories. *Thinking & Reasoning, 4(4),* 353-376.

Hatfield, G. (2013). Psychology, epistemology, and the problem of the external world: Russell and before. In E. H. Reck (ed), *The historical turn in analytical philosophy* (pp. 171-200). London: Palgrave MacMillan.

Hoch, S. J., & Tschirgi, J. E. (1983). Cue redundancy and extra logical inference in a deductive reasoning task. *Memory & Cognition 11,* 200-209.

Hoch, S. J., & Tschirgi, J. E. (1985). Logical knowledge and cue redundancy in deductive reasoning. *Memory & Cognition 13*, 453-462.

Horn, L. R. (2000). From if to iff: Conditional perfection as pragmatic strengthening. *Journal of pragmatics, 32*, 289-326.

Inhelder, B., & Piaget, J. (1958). *The growth of logical thinking from childhood to adolescence.* New York: Basic Books.

Jevons, W. S. (1906). *Logic.* London: Macmillan.

Johnson-Laird, P. N. (2006). *How we reason.* Oxford: Oxford University Press.

Johnson-Laird, P. N., & Bara, B. G. (1984), Syllogistic inference, *Cognition, 16*, 1-61.

Johnson-Laird, P. N., & Byrne, R. M. J. (1991). *Deduction.* Hove, UK: Lawrence Erlbaum Associates Ltd.

Johnson-Laird, P. N., & Savary, F. (1999). Illusory inferences: A novel class of erroneous deductions. *Cognition, 71.* 191-229.

Johnson-Laird, P. N., & Wason, P. C. (1970). Insight into a logical relation. *Quarterly Journal of Experimental Psychology, 22*, 49-61.

Johnson-Laird, P. N., & Wason, P. C. (1977). A theoretical analysis of insight into a reasoning task. In P. N. Johnson-Laird & P. C. Wason (eds), *Thinking: Readings in cognitive science* (pp. 143-157). Cambridge, MA: Cambridge University Press.

Kirby, K. N. (1994). Probabilities and utilities of fictional outcomes in Wason's four-card selection task. *Cognition, 51*, 1–28.

Klauer, K. C., Stahl, C., & Erdfelder, E. (2007). The abstract selection task: New data and an almost comprehensive model, *Journal of Experimental Psychology: Learning, Memory, and Cognition, 33(4)*, 680-703.

Kneale, W., & Kneale, M. (1962). *The Development of Logic.* Oxford: Oxford University Press.

Krzyżanowska, K., Wenmackers, S., & Douven, I. (2013). Inferential conditionals and evidentiality. *Journal of Logic, Language and Information. 22(3)*, 315-334.

Kusch, M. (1995). *Psychologism. A case study in the sociology of philosophical knowledge*. London: Routledge.

Kusch, M. (2014). Psychologism. In E. N. Zalta (ed), *The Stanford Encyclopedia of Philosophy (Spring 2014 Edition)*, URL: http://plato.stanford.edu/archives/spr2014/entries/psychologism/

Legrenzi, P. (1970). Relations between language and reasoning about deductive rules. In G. B. Flores D'Arcais, & W. J. M. Levelt (eds), *Advances in Psycholinguistics* (pp. 322-333). Amsterdam: North-Holland.

Lewis, D. (1976). Probability of conditionals and conditional probabilities. *Philosophical Review, 95*, 581-589.

Manktelow, K. (2012). *Thinking and reasoning: An introduction to the psychology of reason, judgment and decision making*. Hove, UK: Psychology Press.

Manktelow, K., & Over, D. E. (1990). Deontic thought and the selection task. In K. J. Gilhooly, M. T. G. Keane, R. H. Logie, & G. Erdos (eds), *Lines of thinking: Reflections on the psychology of thought* (pp. 153-164). Chichester: Wiley.

Markovits, H. (1985). Incorrect conditional reasoning among adults: Competence or performance? *British Journal of Psychology, 76*, 241-247.

Markovits, H., Fleury, M. L., Quinn, S., & Venet, M. (1998). The development of conditional reasoning and the structure of semantic memory. *Child Development, 69*, 742-755.

Markovits, H., Venet, M., Janveau-Brennan, G., Malfait, N., Pion, N., & Vadeboncoeur, I. (1996). Reasoning in young children: Fantasy and information retrieval. *Child Development 67(6)*, 2857-2872.

Maróth, M. (1983). *Arisztotelésztől Avicennáig*. [From Aristotle to Avicenna]. Budapest, HU: Akadémiai.

Nickerson, R. S., & Butler, S. F. (2008). Efficiency in data gathering: Set-size effects in the selection task. *Thinking & Reasoning, 14(1)*, 60-82.

Novaes, C. D. (2012). *Formal languages in logic. A philosophical and cognitive analysis*. New York: Cambridge University Press.

Nute, D. (2003). Defeasible logic. *Lecture Notes in Computer Science, 2543,* 151-169.

Oaksford, M., & Chater, N. (1994). A rational analysis of the selection task as optimal data selection. *Psychological Review, 101,* 608-631.

Oaksford, M., & Chater, N. (1998). *Rationality in an uncertain world: Essay on the cognitive science of human reasoning.* Hove, UK: Psychology Press.

Oaksford, M., & Chater, N. (2003). Conditional probability and the cognitive science of conditional reasoning. *Mind and Language, 18(4),* 359-379.

Oaksford, M., & Chater, N. (2007). *Bayesian rationality: The probabilistic approach to human reasoning.* Oxford: Oxford University Press.

Oaksford, M., & Chater, N. (2009). Précis of Bayesian rationality: The probabilistic approach to human reasoning. *Behavioral and Brain Sciences, 32,* 69-120.

Oaksford, M., & Chater, N. (2010). Cognition and conditionals: An introduction. In M. Oaksford, & N. Chater (eds), *Cognition and Conditionals. Probability and logic in human thinking* (pp. 3-36). Oxford: Oxford University Press.

Oberauer, K., & Wilhelm, O. (2003). The meaning(s) of conditionals: conditional probabilities, mental models and personal utilities. *Journal of Experimental Psychology: Learning, Memory, and Cognition, 29(4),* 680-693.

O'Brien, D. P., Braine, M. D. S., & Yang, Y. (1994). Propositional reasoning by mental models? Simple to refute in principle and in practice. *Psychological Review, 101,* 711-724.

Pfeifer, N. (2013). The new psychology of reasoning: A mental probability logical perspective. *Thinking & Reasoning, 19(3-4),* 329-345.

Platt, R. D., & Griggs, R. A. (1993). Facilitation in the abstract selection task: The effects of attentional and instructional factors. *Quarterly Journal of Experimental Psychology, 46A(4),* 591-613.

Pollard, P. (1982). Human reasoning: Some possible effects of availability. *Cognition, 12,* 65-96.

Pollard, P., & Evans, J. St. B. T. (1980). The influence of logic on conditional reasoning performance. *Quarterly Journal of Experimental Psychology, 32*, 605-624.

Ramsey, F. P. (1926/1990). Truth and probability. In: D. H. Mellor (ed), *Philosophical papers* (pp. 52-94). Cambridge: Cambridge University Press.

Ramsey, F. P. (1929/1990). General propositions and causality. In: D. H. Mellor (ed), *Philosophical papers* (pp. 145-163). Cambridge: Cambridge University Press.

Read, S. (1995) *Thinking about logic. An introduction to the philosophy of logic.* Oxford: Oxford University Press

Reiter, R. (1980). A logic for default reasoning. *Artificial Intelligence, 13*, 81-132.

Rips, L. J. (1994). *The psychology of proof: deductive reasoning in human thinking.* Cambridge, MA: MIT Press.

Rips, L. J., & Marcus, S. L. (1977). Suppositions and the analysis of conditional sentences. In M. A. Just, & P. A. Carpenter (eds), *Cognitive processes in comprehension* (pp. 185-220), Hillsdale, NJ: Lawrence Erlbaum Associates, Inc.

Roth, E. M. (1979). Facilitating insight in a reasoning task. *British Journal of Psychology, 70*, 265-271.

Rumain, B., Connell, J., & Braine, M. D. (1983). Conversational comprehension processes are responsible for reasoning fallacies in children as well as adults: If is not the biconditional. *Developmental Psychology, 19*, 471-481.

Sanford, D. H. (1989). *If P, then Q. Conditionals and the foundations of reasoning.* London: Routledge.

Shin, S. J., & Lemon, O. (2008). Diagrams. In E. N. Zalta (ed), *Stanford Encyclopedia of Philosophy (Winter 2008 Edition).* URL: http://plato.stanford.edu/archives/win2008/entries/diagrams/

Sperber, D., Cara, F., & Girotto, V. (1995). Relevance theory explains the selection task. *Cognition, 57*, 31-95.

Stahl, C., Klauer, K. C., & Erdfelder, E. (2008). Matching bias in the selection task is not eliminated by explicit negations. *Thinking & Reasoning, 14(3),* 281-303.

Stalnaker, R. C. (1968). A theory of conditionals. In W. L. Harper, R. Stalnaker, & G. Pearce (eds), *Ifs* (pp. 41-55). Dordrecht: D. Reidel.

Stalnaker, R. C. (1976). Indicative conditionals. In W. L. Harper, R. Stalnaker, & G. Pearce (eds), *Ifs* (pp. 193-210). Dordrecht: D. Reidel.

Stenning, K., & Oberlander, J. (1995). A cognitive theory of graphical and linguistic reasoning: Logic and implementation. *Cognitive Science, 19,* 97-140.

Stenning, K., & van Lambalgen, M. (2000). Semantics as a foundation for psychology: A case study of Wason's selection task. *Journal of Logic, Language and Information, 10,* 273-317.

Stenning K., & van Lambalgen M. (2008). *Human reasoning and cognitive science.* Cambridge, MA: MIT Press.

Tarski, A., (1946/1995). *Introduction to logic and to the methodology of deductive sciences.* Mineola, NY: Dover Publications.

Thompson, V. A. (1995). Conditional reasoning: The necessary and sufficient conditions. *Canadian Journal of Experimental Psychology / Revue canadienne de psychologie expérimentale, 49(1),* 1-60.

van Benthem, J. (2008). Logic and reasoning: do the facts matter? *Studia Logica, 88(1),* 67-84.

Veszelka, A. (1999). *Feltételesen plasztikus* [Conditionally pliable]. Master's thesis, ELTE, Hungary.

Veszelka, A. (2007). A feltételes állítás kísérleti vizsgálata: mégis van benne logika? [The experimental investigation of the conditional statement: Does it have logic?]. *Magyar Pszichológiai Szemle 62(4), 475-488.*, English version available upon request.

Wagner-Egger, P. (2007). Conditional reasoning and the Wason selection task: Biconditional interpretation instead of a reasoning bias. *Thinking & Reasoning, 13(4),* 484-505.

Wason, P. C. (1966). Reasoning. In B. M. Foss (ed), *New horizons in psychology* (pp. 135-151). Harmondsworth, UK: Penguin Books.

Wason, P. C. (1968). Reasoning about a rule. *Quarterly Journal of Experimental Psychology, 20,* 273-281.

Wason, P. C. (1969). Regression in reasoning? *British Journal of Psychology, 60,* 471-480.

Wason, P. C. (1970). Psychological aspects of inference. In G. B. Flores D'Arcais, & W. J. M. Levelt (eds), *Advances in Psycholinguistics* (pp. 344-346). Amsterdam: North-Holland.

Wason, P. C., & Green, D. (1984). Reasoning and mental representation. *Quarterly Journal of Experimental Psychology, 36A,* 597-610.

Whitehead, A. N., & Russell, B. (1910-13/1962), *Principa Mathematica,* 2nd ed. Cambridge: Cambridge University Press.

Wilkins, M. C. (1928). The effect of changed material on the ability to do formal syllogistic reasoning. *Archives of Psychology, 102,* 1-83.

Woodworth, R. S., & Schlosberg, H. (1954). *Experimental Psychology,* 2nd ed., New York: Holt, Rinehart & Winston.

Woodworth, R. S., & Sells, S. B. (1935). An atmosphere effect in formal syllogistic reasoning. *Journal of Experimental Psychology, 18(4),* 451-460.

Yama, H. (2001). Matching versus optimal data selection in the Wason selection task. *Thinking & Reasoning, 7,* 295-311.

9 Index

www.ingramcontent.com/pod-product-compliance
Lightning Source LLC
Chambersburg PA
CBHW050122280326
41933CB00010B/1210